Hugo Pinksterboer

Tipbook
Saxophone

Handy, clearly written, and up-to-date.
The reference manual for both beginners and advanced
saxophonists, including Tipcodes and a glossary.

THE **TIPBOOK** COMPANY

THE BEST GUIDE TO YOUR INSTRUMENT!

Thanks

For their information, their expertise, their time, and their help, we'd like to thank the following musicians, teachers, technicians, and other saxophone experts: Terry Landry (Rico International, CA), Tim Brennan, James Grondin (The Woodwind & Brasswind, IN), Ray Chambers (American Band Instrument Service, TX), Roberto Romeo (Roberto's Woodwind, NY), Thierry Lobel (Selmer, France), Candy Dulfer, Hans Dulfer, Leo van Oostrom, Davina Cowan, Fred Leeflang, Josephine van Rosmalen, Gerdie IJland, Hans Jan van der Deure and Paul Kortenhorst (Saxophone Shop), Louis Hummel (Hummel Saxophones), Wim Tober (LVSD/National Association of Saxophone Teachers), Gerard ten Hoedt (Müller Music), Hanneke van der Horst, Willem Pinksterboer, and the late Peter Barkema.

Anything missing?

Any omissions? Any areas that could be improved? Please go to www.tipbook.com to contact us; thanks!

Acknowledgements

Concept, design, and illustrations: Gijs Bierenbroodspot
Cover photo: René Vervloet
Editor: Robert L. Doerschuk
Proofreaders: Nancy Bishop and René de Graaff

IN BRIEF

Have you just started playing the saxophone? Are you thinking about buying a sax, or do you just want to learn more about the one you already have? If so, this book will tell you all you need to know. About buying or renting saxophones, lessons and practicing, play-testing and selecting an instrument, choosing mouthpieces, reeds, and ligatures, maintenance and tuning, about the history and the family of the saxophone, and much more.

The best you can
Having read this Tipbook, you'll be able to get the best out of your saxophone, to buy the best instrument you can, and to easily grasp any other literature on the subject, from books and magazines to catalogs and Internet publications.

Begin at the beginning
If you have just started playing, or haven't yet begun, pay particular attention to the first five chapters. Have you been playing any longer? Then skip ahead to Chapter 6. Please note that all prices mentioned in this book are based on estimated street prices in American dollars.

Glossary
The glossary at the end of the book briefly explains most of the terms you'll come across as a sax player. To make life even easier, it doubles as an index.

Hugo Pinksterboer

CONTENTS

SEE WHAT YOU READ WITH TIPCODE

www.tipbook.com

In addition to the many illustrations on the following pages, Tipbooks offer you a new way to see – and even hear – what you are reading about. The *Tipcodes* that you will come across regularly in this book give you access to extra pictures, short movies, soundtracks, and other additional information at www.tipbook.com.

How it works is very simple. One example: On page 78 of this book you can read about adjusting the underside of a reed. Right above that paragraph it says **Tipcode SAX-013**. Type in that code on the Tipcode page at www.tipbook.com and you will see a short movie that shows you this technique.

Enter code, watch movie
You enter the Tipcode beneath the movie window on the Tipcode page. In most cases, you will then see the relevant images or hear the soundtrack within five to ten seconds. Tipcodes can activate a short movie, sound, or both, or a series of photos.

Tipcodes listed
You can find all the Tipcodes used in this book in a single list on page 124.

Quick start
The movies, photo series, and soundtracks are designed so that they start quickly. If you miss something the first time, you can of course repeat them. And if it all happens too fast, use the pause button below the movie window.

First, make your selection: Tipcode, chords, and fingering charts, or the glossary.

The Tipcode window displays movies, photo series, fingering charts, chords, and explanations of the words used in this book.

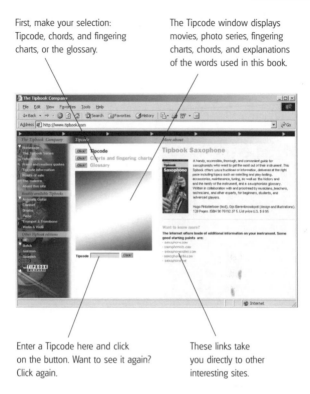

Enter a Tipcode here and click on the button. Want to see it again? Click again.

These links take you directly to other interesting sites.

Plug-ins

If the software you need to view the movies or photos is not yet installed on your computer, you'll automatically be told which software you need, and where you can download it. This kind of software (*plug-ins*) is free.

Still more at www.tipbook.com

You can find even more information at www.tipbook.com. For instance, you can look up words in the glossaries of all the Tipbooks published to date. For saxophonists, clarinetists, and flutists there are fingering charts, for drummers there are the rudiments, and for guitarists and pianists there are chord diagrams. Also included are links to some of the websites mentioned in the *Want to Know More?* section of each Tipbook.

1. A SAXOPHONIST?

As a saxophonist you can play perfect, straight notes, and you can make your instrument whisper, scream, or hiss just as easily. That's one of the main reasons why you hear saxophonists play in a wide variety of musical styles, and in many different types of bands and orchestras.

With a saxophone you can go from jazz to classical music, from Latin to rock and soul. As you can influence the sound of the instrument to a large extent, saxophonists can be equally at home in all those styles.

High school and college bands

Of course, saxophonists are essential in all the various types of high school and college bands: marching bands that perform either onstage, in parades, or during football games; jazz bands; wind bands; or concert bands, which may have some sixty to more than a hundred band members.

Rock, funk, jazz

You can also join the horn section of a rock or funk band, adding spicy riffs or tender harmonies to the music. Saxophone solos are rare in such bands, but they're one of the main features in jazz ensembles. Popular formats are the jazz quartet (saxophone, drums, piano, double bass) or quintet, which usually includes a second saxophonist or a trumpet player.

Very young

You won't find the saxophone in the standard lineup of the symphony orchestra. Why not? Because Beethoven,

Mozart, and numerous other great classical composers were long dead when Adolphe Sax invented the saxophone, around 1840. The other instruments in the symphony orchestra are a lot older.

But you can play it

That's not to say that you can't play music from that era: Lots of compositions have been adapted for sax players. Composers of later date have also written classical music for saxophonists. Some well-known names are Béla Bartók, Hector Berlioz, Maurice Ravel, and Richard Strauss.

Much more

Apart from a wide range of bands and orchestras, there are many other formats for sax players. For example, there are compositions for saxophone solo (just a sax, nothing else); there are duets for sax and piano, or for two saxophones (you can use duets written for oboe or flute too, if you want to play older music!). Also, there is music for saxophone quartets, ranging from jazz and improvised music to hymns, children's songs, and string quartets that have been adapted for saxes. A similar range of works is available for saxophone choirs, a larger type of ensemble.

Just like singing

Saxophone playing is often compared with singing, because the saxophone is almost as versatile and expressive as your own voice. Similarly, it's just as easy to play a saxophone out of tune as it is to sing out of tune… So when you learn to play the instrument, you'll also have to learn to tell whether you play in tune.

Alto and tenor   Tipcode SAX-001

Saxophones come in various sizes or *voices*. The *alto saxophone* and the larger, lower-sounding *tenor saxophone* are the most widely used. Their sounds suit all kinds of music, and they're easier to master than the other voices. Most players start on one of these horns.

Soprano and baritone

The next two popular saxes are the small, high-pitched *soprano*, and the big, low-pitched *baritone*. Saxophone players often specialize in one of the four voices – but they

A tenor (left) and an alto saxophone.

usually play two or more of them.

And more

There are even more saxophones; you'll find the others in Chapter 12, *The Family*. As different as they may appear, all saxophones are basically the exact same instrument, with the exact same arrangement of keys. It's only the sizes that differ.

Saxes and horns

As 'saxophone' is quite a long word, most saxophonists talk about their 'sax' instead. Likewise, some musicians say 'saxist' rather than saxophonist. Many sax players call their instrument a 'horn' – just like trumpeters and other brass players often do.

2. A QUICK TOUR

With all of those keys and rods, a saxophone looks more complicated than it really is. In this chapter you will see which parts make up a saxophone, what they're called and what they're for.

Each saxophone has basically the same set of parts, whether it's a soprano, an alto, a tenor, or a baritone. In this chapter, the alto saxophone is pictured. You'll find the others in the next chapter, *Four Saxes*.

Tube with holes

Essentially, a saxophone is a long tube with holes in it. Just as on a recorder, you play the lowest note by closing off all of those *toneholes*. If you open the last hole, the tone goes up: You'll play a higher pitch. If you then open the next tonehole, the pitch is raised again – and so on.

The keys

The toneholes of a saxophone are too far apart, and most of them are far too big, to cover them with your fingertips.

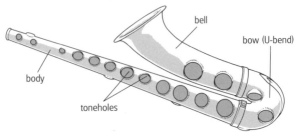

A saxophone body and bell without its keys:
a long tube full of holes.

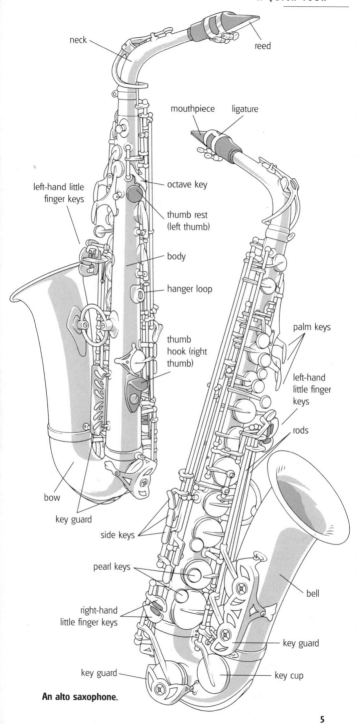

neck

reed

mouthpiece

ligature

octave key

thumb rest (left thumb)

left-hand little finger keys

body

hanger loop

palm keys

left-hand little finger keys

thumb hook (right thumb)

rods

bow

key guard

side keys

pearl keys

bell

right-hand little finger keys

key guard

key guard

key cup

An alto saxophone.

5

Besides, there are more toneholes than you have fingers. That's why the instrument has *keys* to open and close them.

Body, neck, and bell

The largest part of a saxophone, covered with keys and rods, is the *body*. At the top end you'll find the *neck*. The wide flaring part at the other end is the *bell*.

Mouthpiece and reed

Attached to the neck is the *mouthpiece* with the *reed*. This reed, a thin piece of cane, is what generates the saxophone sound. A *ligature* holds the reed in place.

Sound

When you talk or sing, your vocal chords vibrate. This makes the air around them vibrate, and that's what sound is: vibrating air. When you are playing the sax, you make the reed vibrate, and with it the air column in the saxophone.

Long tube, low notes

If you close all the toneholes, the saxophone will sound its lowest note: The sax 'tube' is at its longest. To play higher notes, you open one or more toneholes. The more toneholes you open, the higher notes will sound.

Pads

In order for a sax to play well, its keys should properly close the toneholes, without any air leaking. Therefore, the *key cups* that stop the toneholes are fitted with *pads*. These felt discs, covered with thin, soft leather, seal the toneholes.

Resonators

In the middle of each pad is a small metal or plastic disc. These *resonators* make the instrument sound a little brighter.

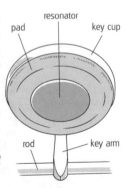

Wider and wider

The body of the sax becomes wider as it progresses from the neck to the bell. In technical terms, saxophones have a *conical shape* – like an ice-cream cone.

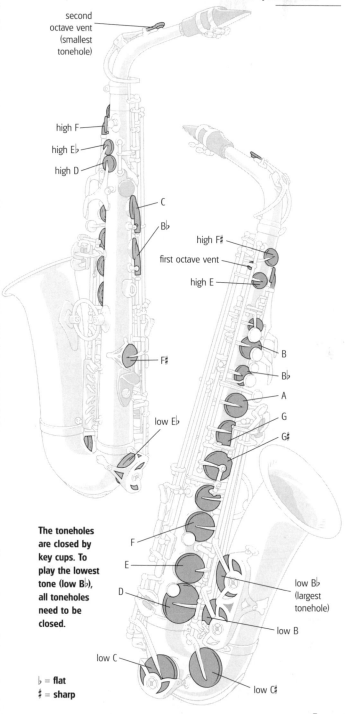

second octave vent (smallest tonehole)

high F

high E♭

high D

C

B♭

high F♯

first octave vent

high E

B

B♭

F♯

A

G

G♯

low E♭

The toneholes are closed by key cups. To play the lowest tone (low B♭), all toneholes need to be closed.

F

E

D

low B♭ (largest tonehole)

low B

low C

low C♯

♭ = **flat**
♯ = **sharp**

7

Bigger and bigger

As the saxophone gets wider, the toneholes get bigger. The smallest tonehole is on the neck: It's the neck *octave vent*. The largest tonehole is located at the opposite end of the horn, in the bell. Some consider the bell itself to be the largest tonehole: That's where the lowest note comes from.

Nine digits, twenty-five keys

The key system allows you to open and close all of the sax's twenty-four or twenty-five toneholes with just eight fingers and a thumb.

Springs

When you're not playing, about half of the keys are open; the others are closed. Each key has a *needle spring*, which makes sure the key closes again after you've opened it, or the other way around.

Felts and corks

Small felt and cork *bumpers* prevent the moving metal parts from producing too much noise. They also help some keys open and close simultaneously, and determine how far some of the keys open.

Key guards

Key guards protect some of the most vulnerable key cups from getting damaged.

Thumb hook, thumb rest

Your right thumb, placed under the *thumb hook*, helps support the instrument. Your left thumb, placed on the *thumb rest*, operates the *octave key*.

Hanger loop

Saxophones are supported by a neckstrap or *sling*. The *hanger loop* for the strap hook is about halfway up the back of the body.

THE KEYS

Sax players use many different names for the keys of their instrument. What one calls a pearl key is a finger pad to the next, for example. Following are some of the main names.

The system
The entire system of keys, springs, rods, and other moving parts, is referred to as the *keywork, key system, mechanism,* or *action.*

Keys and key cups
Technically speaking, keys are the things you press to open or close a tonehole, while the key cups or *pad cups* actually stop the toneholes. Most saxophonists, however, use the word *key* for the entire system, from key to key cup.

Easy
The complex-looking mechanism becomes a lot easier to understand if you just look at the keys your fingers rest on, as shown on page 11. To complete the picture, you'll find all the key cups and the corresponding notes on page 7.

Pearl keys
The front side of the sax has eight round keys with a mother-of-pearl or (imitation) shell inlay. They're usually referred to as *pearl keys, key pearls,* or *pearls.* Some horns have shell inlays on other keys as well.

Little finger keys
Your left little finger operates no less than four keys. This takes a bit of practice, in the beginning. Your right little finger controls two similar keys. The rollers between the keys make it easier to slide your pinkie from one key to the other.

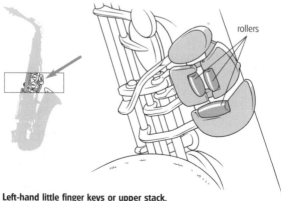

rollers

Left-hand little finger keys or upper stack.

9

Alternative names

The little finger keys are also known as *table keys* or *touch plates*. The groups of two (right hand) and four (left hand) keys are known as the *lower* and *upper stack*, respectively, and as (*floating rocker*) *tables*, *plateaus*, or *clusters*.

Side and palm keys   Tipcode SAX-002

On the right-hand side you'll find four or five rectangular keys, the *side keys*. On the top left-hand side, there are three *palm keys*, so called because you can play them with the palm of your hand. These two sets of keys are mostly used for playing high notes and trills.

Spatulas

Due to their shape, the front F key, and the side and palm keys are also known as *spatula keys* or *spatulas*. The little finger keys are sometimes referred to as spatulas too. Keys with a lever-type action are known as *levers*.

KEYS AND NOTES

On a piano, there's a key for every note. On a saxophone, it's very different: For most notes, you need a combination of keys. That makes it hard to add note names to the keys.

Londeix

Still, it's useful to be able to identify them. Over the years, a number of systems have been developed for this purpose. One of the most common, conceived by the French saxophonist Jean Marie Londeix, is pictured on the opposite page.

Keys 1 to 8

The keys 1 to 6 are played with your right and left index, middle, and ring fingers. Your right little finger operates key 7 (for the low C) and the key for the low E-flat (E♭). Your left little finger operates key 8, on the lower stack.

Octave key   Tipcode SAX-003

Key O, on the back, is the octave key. If you play, say, a low G, and then press the octave key, you will hear a G that sounds an *octave* higher (eight white notes on a piano keyboard).

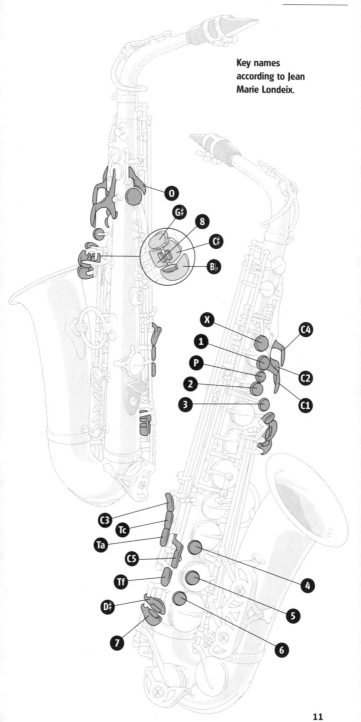

Key names according to Jean Marie Londeix.

Two vents

The octave key opens and closes two vents. The upper one is on the neck, clearly visible. The lower octave vent is on the body, between the high E and F♯ key cups (see page 7). You don't need to worry about which one to open for the note you're playing: You just operate the octave key, and the system automatically opens the right vent.

The very highest

Keys C1 through C5 are for the highest notes. The higher the number, the higher the pitch of the note. C5 is for high F-sharp (F♯). Not all saxophones have this key (see page 39).

Trills and more

The keys named with a T are used to play trills, but not only that. One example? With Tc you can, of course, also just play a C. As for the trills:

- With Tc you can trill between B and C.
- With Tf you can trill between F and F♯.
- With Ta you can trill between A and B♭.

F = X

Key X, also known as *front F*, *quick F*, or *forked F*, can be used to reach not only high F, but also high E and F♯ in certain passages.

Fingering charts

Most notes can be played with various fingerings. *Fingering charts*, available on the Internet and in many saxophone books, show you exactly which combination(s) of keys to use to play any given note. You can also find saxophone fingering charts at www.tipbook.com.

THE REGISTERS

The octave key is also known as the *register key*. You use it to go from the lowest series of notes you can play (the low register) to the next, higher-sounding series (the middle register).

Fingering chart.
By pressing the two shaded keys, you'll finger an A.

Three registers

Some saxophonists divide the range of the instrument into three registers: low, middle, and upper. Without the octave key, you're in the low register. The middle register involves the same notes, played *with* the octave key. Adding keys C1 to C5 brings you to the upper register.

Five registers

Other players say there are five registers, with the *bottom register* referring to the lowest four notes (B♭, B, C, and C♯). The difference between the *lower* and the *upper register,* both played using the six pearl keys only, is the use of the octave key. The upper or *top register* is played using C1 to C5. The very highest notes of the *altissimo register* are played using *harmonics* or *top tones,* which require special fingerings and air stream adjustments.

3. FOUR SAXES

If you go to a store and ask for a saxophone, you will be asked which voice you want: an alto, or a tenor, or perhaps a soprano or a baritone? This chapter introduces you to these four voices, their sound, and their ranges – and it explains why a C is not always a C.

From a distance, you might say that a baritone sax looks nothing like a soprano sax. However, they are basically the same instruments. The baritone is just bigger, and thus lower in pitch.

Soprano   Tipcode SAX-005
Because of its size, the high-sounding soprano sax is easy to handle. Sopranos are usually not recommended for beginning players, however, as these smaller horns are harder to play in tune than altos or tenors. Traditionally, sopranos have a straight body, but curved sopranos are available too.

Alto   Tipcode SAX-006
The alto sax is a better choice for beginners. It's easier to play in tune than a soprano, and easier to handle than a tenor. The alto is at home in pretty much any style of music, and there's more classical music written for the alto than for any of the other saxes. In concert and marching bands, too, the alto is a very popular choice.

Tenor   Tipcode SAX-007
The tenor is the most widely used sax in jazz, but you'll find it in other styles as well. The sound could be described as warmer, fatter, juicier, or richer than that of an alto or a

Soprano saxophone.

Alto saxophone.

soprano. It's also more versatile: You can make a tenor sound anywhere from piercing and edgy to soft as a whisper. Together with the alto, the tenor is the best choice for beginning players.

Baritone

Tipcode SAX-008

The baritone sax or *bari* is the largest of the four. To make it manageable, it has its typical looped neck and a 'tall' bell. If not, it would be over seven feet long. The baritone, with

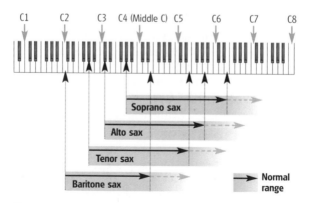

The ranges of the four most popular saxophones.

Tenor saxophone.

Baritone saxophone.

its big, fat tone, sounds an octave lower than the alto. It's not a great horn for beginners, due to its size and price.

HOW HIGH, HOW LOW?   Tipcode SAX-009

The normal range of a saxophone is about two and a half octaves. Good players can stretch it to three or four octaves, or even further.

Same note, different timbre   Tipcode SAX-010

There are at least fourteen notes that can be played on all four saxophones: from the A♭ below Middle C (A♭3), up to the next A (A4). If you play these pitches on the four saxophone voices, you'll hear – literally – four different voices, each with its own timbre or tone.

TRANSPOSING INSTRUMENTS

If you play the piano, and your chart shows a C, you play the C key and you'll hear a C. If a saxophone chart shows a C, you finger a C, but you will hear a different note. This is because saxophones are *transposing instruments*.

Concert instruments

Pianos, guitars, and many other instruments are called *concert instruments*, because they sound in *concert pitch*: The note you play is the note you hear. With transposing instruments, this is different.

E♭ instruments

If you finger a C on an alto or a baritone, for example, you will hear an E♭ (E-flat). These two saxes are *E♭ instruments*.

B♭ instruments

If you finger a C on a soprano or a tenor, you will hear a B♭ (B-flat). These two saxes are *B♭ instruments*.

Same fingerings   Tipcode SAX-011

This may sound a little complicated at first, but it has one great advantage: No matter which sax you're playing, you always use the same fingerings. For example, a Middle C on paper *always* means that you close the six pearl keys + key 7 (right little finger). The note that comes out is the note the composer wanted to hear.

The note C5 on paper, the corresponding fingering C for all saxes, and the resulting concert pitches.

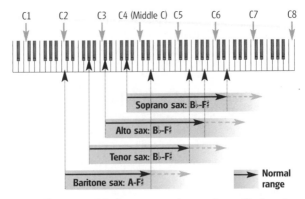

Again: The ranges of the four most popular saxophones. The lowest note on a soprano (B♭) sounds an A♭ on the piano; the lowest note on an alto (also B♭) sounds a D♭ on the piano, and so on.

Transposed parts

So a saxophonist's part doesn't tell you which pitches to play, but which notes to finger: Saxophonists read *transposed parts*. When you play your part, your instrument 'transposes' the written note to the pitch the composer had in mind. If you're playing an alto and the composer wants to hear a concert E♭, you'll find a C in your part. If a tenor is supposed to sound an E♭, the part will show an F.

Saxophones in C

Wouldn't it be much easier if saxophones sounded in C, like pianos? Yes, but making a saxophone in another tuning would also change its timbre. A tenor saxophone in C, for example, would be smaller than the tenor in B♭. Due to this smaller size, its sound would tend toward that of an alto.

Alto in C?

An alto couldn't be made to sound in C at all: It would have to be smaller than a soprano – or almost as big as a tenor… That said, saxophones in C and other tunings have been made (see pages 104–105), but the E♭ and B♭ instruments have outlasted them.

Other wind instruments

Incidentally, saxes are not the only transposing instruments. Most trumpets and clarinets, for example, are in B♭, just like the soprano and tenor saxes; alto flutes are in G, and French horns in F and B♭.

4. LEARNING TO PLAY

It doesn't take much time to learn to play the saxophone, but it takes quite a lot of time to learn how to play it well – to play it in tune, and to develop a good sound. A chapter about some of the main elements of learning the instrument, and about taking lessons, and practicing.

It's not the complicated-looking mechanism that takes so much time to learn. After all, it was devised to make playing the saxophone as easy as possible.

Good sound
It will take you longer to make the instrument sound the way you want it to sound: A saxophone only sounds as good as the person who plays it. First of all, playing a wind instrument is more than blowing air through a tube. To sound good, you need a good breathing technique. Good air stream control is also important for being able to play in tune – and to play long phrases, of course.

Embouchure
The second important element for your sound is how you use your lips, jaws, tongue, and all the muscles around them. Altogether that is known as the *embouchure*. This term is based on the French word for mouth, *bouche*.

LESSONS
A good saxophone teacher covers everything that has to do with playing the instrument – from developing air

stream control and embouchure to playing in tune, and from reading music to good posture.

Locating a teacher

Looking for a private teacher? Music stores may have teachers on staff, or they can refer you to one. You can also consult your local Musicians' Union, or the band director at a high school. Some players have found great teachers in musicians that they caught at a performance. You may also check the classified ads in newspapers, in music magazines, or on supermarket bulletin boards, or consult the *Yellow Pages*. Professional private teachers will usually charge between twenty-five and seventy-five dollars per hour. Some make house calls, which will cost you extra.

Group or individual lessons

Instead of taking individual lessons, you can also go for group lessons if that's an option in your area. Private lessons are more expensive, but can be tailored exactly to your needs.

Collectives

You also may want to check whether there are any teachers' collectives or music schools in your vicinity. These collectives may offer extras such as ensemble playing, master classes, and clinics, in a wide variety of styles and at various levels.

Questions, questions

On your first visit to a teacher, don't ask only how much it costs. Here are some other questions.

- Is a free **introductory lesson** included? This is a good way to find out how well you get on with the teacher, and, for that matter, with the instrument.
- Is the teacher interested in taking you on as a student if you are just doing it **for the fun of it**, or are you expected to practice at least three hours a day?
- Do you have to make a large investment in method books right away, or is **course material provided**?
- Can you **record your lessons**, so that you can listen at home to how you sound, and once more to what has been said?

- Are you allowed to fully concentrate on **the style of music you want to play**, or will you be required – or stimulated! – to learn other styles?
- Is this teacher going to make you **practice scales** for two years, or will you be pushed onto a stage as soon as possible?

PRACTICING

What goes for every instrument especially goes for wind instruments: It's better to practice half an hour every day than a couple of hours twice a week. This is especially true because of your embouchure. If you don't play for a few days, your embouchure will suffer straight away.

Three times ten

If you find it hard to practice half an hour a day, try dividing it up into two quarter-hour sessions, or three of ten minutes each.

The right pitch

On a saxophone, the notes you finger do not sound in pitch automatically: They can easily sound a bit *flat* (too low) or *sharp* (high). Therefore, you have to learn how to play the notes at the right pitch by using your embouchure and air stream control. The more you play, the faster you will learn to hear whether you are voicing them properly.

Neighbors

If neighbors or housemates are bothered by your practice sessions, it can be enough to simply agree to fixed practice times. If you really play a lot, consider soundproofing a room – even a large cupboard can be big enough. There are books available on sound insulation, or you can hire a specialized contractor, and sometimes it's easiest to go practice someplace else.

Mutes and towels

Most saxophone mutes (a padded ring – or an ordinary towel – that you insert into the bell) aren't very effective. They make the lowest notes difficult to play, while higher notes will hardly be dampened at all: Their toneholes are still wide open.

Pack it up

A more effective alternative is a special bag that completely covers the instrument, considerably cutting down the volume. You play the horn using the three openings of the bag: one for each hand, and one for your mouthpiece.

Your own ears

If you are playing in a loud band, or if you're practicing at full volume in a small space, consider using ear protection. Basic earplugs and earmuffs effectively cut down the volume, but playing in tune and working on your sound becomes really hard: This type of protection makes your instrument and the rest of the band sound as if they're next door. A better but more expensive solution is to use ear protectors that have (preferably adjustable or customized) filters.

Baby teeth and braces

The youngest saxophone players may be hindered when they start losing their baby teeth: If you don't have all your teeth, the instrument may wobble in your mouth. Usually braces aren't that much of a problem, although if you play for a particularly long time, a lower brace might start giving you some trouble.

Play-along CDs

Playing with others is usually more fun than practicing alone – and you don't need to invite a band or an orchestra for that purpose: There are all kinds of CDs available to play along to, in all kinds of styles, for beginners as well as for advanced saxophonists. Your own part is left off, leaving the other musicians for you to play with.

Computer lessons

If you have a computer handy, you can also use special CD-ROMs to practice with. Some feature entire orchestras: You can decide for yourself how fast you want a piece to be played, and which parts you want to hear. There is also software that allows you to slow down difficult phrases on CDs, so you can find out what's going on at your own tempo.

Metronome

Most pieces of music are supposed to be played at a steady

tempo. Practicing with a *metronome* helps you to do so. A metronome is a small mechanical or electronic device that ticks or bleeps out a steady adjustable pulse, so you can tell immediately if you're dragging or speeding.

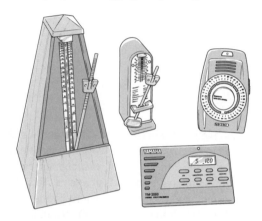

Two mechanical metronomes and two electronic ones.

Record your lessons

If you record your saxophone lessons, you can listen to what was said, and especially to how you sounded when you get home. You can learn a lot by listening carefully to yourself playing. That's why many musicians record themselves when they are practicing too. All you need is a cassette recorder with a built-in microphone. Better equipment (a minidisc recorder with a separate microphone, for instance) is more expensive, but the recordings are usually more enjoyable to listen to.

Listen and play

And finally, visit festivals, concerts, and sessions. One of the best ways to learn to play is seeing other musicians at work. Living legends or local amateurs – every concert's a learning experience. And the best way to learn to play? Play a lot!

5. BUYING A SAX

A saxophone is not the cheapest instrument to start off with, due to its complicated keywork, for one thing. On the other hand: the very best saxophones are quite affordable, compared to other instruments. This chapter covers everything you need to know before you get yourself a saxophone, rented or purchased, new or secondhand. How to go about selecting and play-testing an instrument is covered in Chapter 6, *A Good Sax.*

A basic new alto sax easily costs about a thousand dollars, and a tenor even a bit more. Why so much? Because making a decent sax is a time-consuming affair.

Professional instruments
Professional altos start around three thousand dollars, though you may find instruments with this label for less money. The most expensive altos are about twice this price, and sometimes even more. Tenor prices are usually five to ten percent higher.

Sopranos and baritones
A soprano often costs more than an alto or a tenor of comparable quality: Because of its small size, it's harder to make a soprano that plays both well and in tune. Baritones do not come cheap, due to their size and because fewer of them are made. Bari prices start around two thousand dollars, going up to about seven.

See and hear
To the casual viewer, professional saxes look just like

affordable models. To *see* the differences you'll need to take a close look. To *hear* the differences you have to be a pretty good player. In other words: You can enjoy playing a decent student saxophone for quite a few years.

Time and effort

So why pay more? More expensive saxophones have more time and effort put into them, and higher quality materials are used; they have a better mechanism, stronger rods, better springs, or adjustable keys, and ornamental engravings, or a silver or gold plating rather than a lacquer finish. Making them often involves more handwork, as well as research and development.

A better sound

As a result, a more expensive horn will usually sound better, and it's very likely to be more reliable and easier to play in tune, and to last and stay in adjustment longer than a budget instrument. Also, higher quality instruments generally have higher resale values.

Maintenance, reeds...

In addition to the price you pay for the horn and a case or bag, you have to save some money for the required maintenance (see pages 100–101) and for reeds, of course. You can also invest in your instrument, for example by buying a better mouthpiece, or a new neck – which is worthwhile only if you and your instrument are good enough.

THE SHOP

A saxophone is a precision instrument that needs to be properly maintained and adjusted. Even new saxophones usually need to be adjusted before they play well. That's why you're best off buying your instrument in a shop that has trained technicians on staff. Then you know that they know what they are doing, and that they probably won't send you home with an inferior, badly adjusted instrument.

Check-up

Every saxophone needs periodic check-ups (COA: cleaning, oiling, adjusting). If you have bought a new instrument, that service may be free the first time.

Another store

When you're going to buy an instrument, it can't do any harm to visit a few different stores. Every shop has its own sound, and you'll hear different stories and opinions depending on where you go. Also, not all shops stock the same brands.

Time and space

The more saxes there are to choose from, the harder the choice can be – but the better your chances of finding the one you're looking for. Be sure to take your time, and remember that it's better to come back another time than to play an hour or more in a row. Some stores have separate rooms for play-testing, so that you don't bother the other customers – or vice versa.

On approval

In some cases you may be able to take an instrument on approval, so that you can assess it at your leisure. This is more common with pro-level saxes than cheap ones, and you are more likely to be given the option if you're a good player than if you are choosing your first instrument. An advantage of trying out a saxophone at home is that you are used to how your own instrument sounds there, which helps you to compare properly. In a store everything sounds different – even your own instrument.

Not the same

Even two 'identical' saxophones will never sound exactly the same. So always buy the instrument you think sounds best, and not an 'identical' one from the stockroom. The same goes for mouthpieces.

Another player

In order to hear the differences between one sax and another, you need to be able to play well, which can be a problem if you're going to buy your first instrument. So take someone with you who can play, or find stores where someone on the staff can.

Buying online

You can also buy saxophones online or by mail order. This makes it impossible to compare instruments, but most online and mail-order companies offer a return service for most or all of their products: If you're not happy with it, you can send it back within a certain period of time. Of course the instrument should be in new condition when you send it back.

RENTING

Rather than buying one, you can rent a saxophone. Expect to pay around twenty-five to fifty dollars a month. Usually, there's a minimum rental period – three months, for instance, or a school year. The rental fee is usually set as a percentage of the retail price of the instrument. It also depends on what it covers: Always ask if you get a new or a used (rental-return) instrument, and if insurance and maintenance are included. Stores may ask for a deposit, or require your credit card details.

... and then buying

Some shops offer a rent-to-own program, where all or part of the rental fee you've been paying will be deducted if you decide to buy the instrument in the end. Alternatively, you may get a discount on a new instrument, after the rental period. The longer you've been renting, the larger the discount will be. These are just two of the many variations you may encounter. Always carefully read the contract before signing it. Some stores have contracts that are relatively long and hard to understand. Generally the less verbiage, the fewer loopholes for you to get caught in.

SECONDHAND INSTRUMENTS

Are secondhand saxophones much cheaper? Not always. A decent used instrument can easily cost as much as a new student model – but you can get great used horns, made thirty, forty years ago or more, for less than a new saxophone of similar quality.

Overhaul

Before a saxophone can be sold again, it often needs a partial or complete overhaul, which has its effect on the price of the horn. Still, a secondhand modern instrument will be cheaper than the same one out of the box, of course.

Vintage horns

Jazz players often prefer vintage saxophones, because they feel they sound richer, fatter, and warmer than instruments made in recent years. Some examples of vintage or classic horns are mentioned in Chapter 14, *Brands*. If you're looking for one, it's good to know that there are specialized vintage saxophone stores.

For beginners?

There are also great vintage horns for less money. Note, however, that not every old horn is a good one, and that old horns may be harder to play than new ones. There's more about this on pages 56–57.

The differences: left, an alto built by the inventor, Adolphe Sax, from 1864. Right, a modern alto: more keys, and a bit larger.

Privately or in a store

Secondhand saxophones are sold through music stores, and they're offered for sale in the classified sections in newspapers, on bulletin boards in stores, and on the Internet. If you buy an instrument through an ad, you may pay less than in a store.

In a music store

All the same, buying from a music store does have advantages. The instrument may have been checked and adjusted, and it may come with a warranty; you can go back if you have any questions; you may be able to choose between a number of instruments, and in some cases you can even exchange the sax you bought for a different one, within a certain period. Another advantage: A good store will never charge you much more than an instrument is worth. Private sellers might, either because they don't know better or because they think you don't.

Take someone along

If you go to buy a secondhand saxophone, it's even more important to take along an advanced player who knows about the instrument – especially if you're going to buy privately. Otherwise you might turn down a decent sax just because it doesn't look good, or get saddled with an instrument that looks great but doesn't sound good or play in tune. Technical tips on buying secondhand instruments can be found on pages 52–56.

Appraisal

If you want to be sure you're not paying too much, get the instrument appraised first. An expert technician or salesperson can tell you what it's worth, whether it needs any work done, and what that's going to cost you. If the seller is unwilling to allow this, that could be a warning sign of serious problems.

Sieve

Many decent saxes in disrepair can be made to sound good, even if they leak like a sieve and you can barely get a sound out of them. If you buy an instrument like this, you should be aware that it can easily cost you hundreds of dollars to get it fixed.

AND FINALLY...

The most beautiful sax sound is often that of your favorite sax player. So should you buy the same horn? Not necessarily. Even if you play exactly the same sax, mouthpiece, and reed, you'll still sound different.

Who's blowing the horn

Have one saxophonist play a couple of different saxes, and you will hear pretty much the same sound each time. Have two players play the same sax, and they will sound as different as they always do. In other words: The sound depends more on the player than on the instrument.

More to read

If you want to be well-informed before you go out to buy or rent an instrument, get hold of as many saxophone brochures and catalogs as you can find, along with the price lists. There are also various magazines that offer reviews and other articles on the instrument. Quite a few saxophone books are available too, as well as loads of information on the Internet. You'll find titles, addresses, and other information beginning on page 125.

Fairs and conventions

One last tip: If a music trade show or convention is being held in your area, check it out. Besides lots of instruments you can try out and compare, you will come across plenty of product specialists, as well as numerous fellow sax players who are always a good source of information and inspiration.

6. A GOOD SAX

At first glance, all alto saxophones look alike. And all tenors too. Yet they'll feel different when you play them, and they will sound different, and some have extra keys or other special features. This chapter tells you about those differences, and offers tips for play-testing saxophones and evaluating their sound.

The mouthpiece and the reed are of major influence on how a sax plays and sounds. Both are discussed separately in Chapters 7 and 8.

This chapter
Why two 'identical' saxes can sound and play so differently is linked to all kinds of things. This chapter begins with the instrument's finish and body. The next main subjects discussed are the neck (page 36), the key system (page 39), ergonomics (42), springs and adjustment (44), the pads (45), and secondhand and vintage instruments (52).

Your ears
If you prefer to select a sax using your ears alone, then go straight to the tips for listening and play-testing, which begin on page 47.

Various experts
Sax players rarely agree about anything. The following chapters won't tell you who is right, or what is best, but rather what various experts think about different issues. You'll discover whom you agree with only by playing and by listening – to saxophones, and to saxophonists.

Prices

The price indications mentioned in this chapter refer to altos and tenors, unless specified otherwise.

THE FINISH

Nearly all saxes are made of brass. However, they belong to the family of woodwind instruments, just like the clarinet, the oboe, and other instruments (see Chapter 12). As unfinished brass stains easily and makes your hands smell, most saxophones are finished in one way or another. Apart from the cosmetic aspect, the finish may also have a – very slight – effect on the instrument's sound.

Lacquer

Most saxophones are finished with a glossy, transparent lacquer, which often has a shade of gold (*gold lacquer*).

Silver

Silver-plated instruments are usually said to sound a bit brighter: The silver plating is thinner than lacquer, so it has less of a muffling effect. Some brands offer instruments both in lacquered and silver-plated versions, the latter easily costing two to six hundred dollars extra.

Gold

Gold-plated saxes are rare. They're often said to sound slightly warmer than silver-plated instruments. Gold plating is more expensive than silver plating, and it's quite vulnerable, gold being so soft.

Nickel

Nickel-plated saxes were commonly built well into the 1960s. Some student instruments still have nickel-plated keys, as nickel is relatively inexpensive and durable, and requires little maintenance. Its main drawback is that many people are allergic to it.

Colored saxophones

A few companies sell colored saxophones with a choice of colors and designs, or featuring more durable black nickel plating. A colored finish may cost you an extra three to six hundred dollars.

Matte and unfinished

At the other end of the spectrum there are instruments with a matte finish (often referred to as *hand-brushed*), and there are even unfinished horns.

More than one

Many instruments feature more than one finish: silver-plated keys and a lacquered body, for example, or glossy keys on a matte body.

Engravings

Many saxes have a design, the brand name, and the series name engraved on the bell, and some have engravings elsewhere too. A few brands offer non-engraved horns as an option. Engravings can be made by hand, or using a laser.

Saxophone engraving on the bell (Yamaha).

THE BODY

When it comes to sound, the instrument's exact dimensions are far more important than its finish. The material the body is made of plays a role too.

Brass

Most saxophones are made of *yellow brass*. Some instruments have a distinctive red shade, as they're made of brass with a higher copper content (c. 85%, rather than c. 70%). While some say that this makes the instrument sound brighter, others hear a warmer timbre.

Solid silver or gold

Similarly, a solid silver body is usually said to produce extra brightness, clarity, and projection or 'carrying power,' while other saxophone experts and players claim the opposite. These varying opinions have as much to do with how people experience sound as with the words they choose to describe it. Solid gold saxophones – rare as they are – are typically said to have a 'rich', warm, round, and homogenous sound.

The bore

When you play, the air column inside the saxophone vibrates. It's only logical that the exact shape of that column (the *bore* – the internal dimensions of the body) has a lot of influence on the timbre of the instrument. For example, vintage instruments are said to sound the way they do partially because of a narrower bore. The smaller bore also increases their blowing resistance.

Hard to tell

Other than that, it's nearly impossible to compare saxophones by examining the dimensions of their bores: Being conical (*i.e.*, widening) all the way, differences are hard to tell or to measure. This explains why so much less is written and known about this specific feature than about alloys, finishes, and other factors that are often less decisive for the instrument's sound.

Curved or straight sopranos

Traditionally, soprano saxophones have a straight body, but some brands offer curved models too. Curved sopranos are often said to have a milder, fuller sound, which is closer to the timbre of the other saxophones than the sound of a straight soprano.

Curved or straight necks

Many sopranos, especially in the higher price range, come with both a curved and a straight neck. The words used to describe the difference in sounds produced by curved and straight necks are often similar to the ones mentioned above: Curved necks are usually said to promote a darker, fuller, warmer, milder tone. Conversely, sopranos with straight necks tend to sound brighter and edgier.

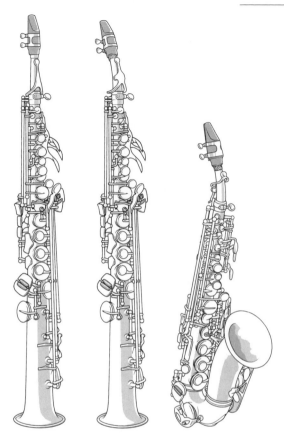

A straight soprano with a straight neck, one with a curved neck, and a curved soprano.

Less tiresome

A different consideration is that a soprano with a curved neck is a bit less tiresome to play: To have your mouthpiece at the required angle, a straight soprano with a straight neck should be held close to horizontal. The curved soprano, in that respect, is the more comfortable horn to play, and it 'feels' most like the other saxophones.

Two more

Two more thoughts? Some players think that straight sopranos often have better *intonation* than curved models, meaning that they're usually easier to play in tune – but note that sopranos are always harder to play in tune than larger saxes. One of the reasons some saxophonists prefer

curved horns is that you can hear yourself better when you play, as the bell doesn't point away from your ears.

Straight altos and tenors

A few brands make straight altos and tenors. Most of what has been said above applies to these instruments as well.

THE NECK

The closer a part is to your mouth, the larger its influence on the way you play and sound. This is what makes mouthpieces and reeds so important – and necks too.

Two necks

Some tenors and altos come with two necks, with different bores, finishes, or both. Usually one neck has a mellower tone, the other sounding a bit brighter. Swapping necks can help you to adapt your sound to the acoustics of the venue you're playing (a 'hard' room requiring a mellower tone, for instance), to the style of music, or your role in the group (playing lead or section, for example).

A straight alto sax.

Finish and bore

As necks are so important, their finish may affect your tone more than the finish elsewhere on the instrument. Some examples: Black-nickeled necks are said to offer the brightest sound, followed by silver-plated, lacquered, and unfinished necks. Remember, however, that the bore and construction of the neck will be more important than its finish or material.

Much to improve

While most horns perform well with the neck they're sold with, you may be able to improve an instrument by providing it with another one. A better neck can enhance almost every aspect of the horn, from timbre and response to intonation.

Prices

An intermediate saxophone may already benefit from a two-hundred-dollar neck, and if you and your sax are good enough, you may want to spend a lot more on a seamless solid sterling silver neck, for example.

Expert required

Necks and saxophones do not always match. The end of the neck, the *tenon*, should of course fit the body's neck receiver – but that's not all. For example, the neck octave vent should be in the right place relative to the rest of the instrument, to prevent intonation problems. In other words: Choosing another neck usually requires consulting a saxophone expert. One more tip: Another neck may require another mouthpiece. The two are closely interrelated, just like mouthpieces and reeds.

Reinforced necks

Reinforced (tenor) necks are available, and they can be custom-made too. Generally speaking, the added mass will make for a less resonant but more focused, tighter sound.

TONEHOLES, POSTS, AND THE BELL

The more you look at saxophones, the easier it'll be to spot differences in the way they're made. Comparing a very expensive horn to the cheapest one in the store will help you to learn to appreciate these differences. Check, for example, the key guards and the way they're attached; have a look at the *bell brace* (the connection between the bell and the body), and compare other details. Often, student instruments have less delicate ornaments and parts than

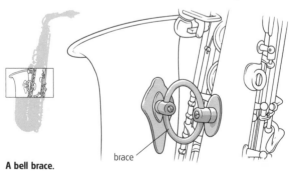

brace

A bell brace.

pro horns. As a result, they may look like they're sturdier, while in reality pro horns will usually outlast cheaper models.

Tonehole edges

Run your finger along the edges of the toneholes. The smoother and thicker they are, the less they will cut into the pads, reducing the chance of leaks. The tonehole edges should be level as well, but that is hard to check. Very few brands still make saxes with rolled tonehole edges, which are very pad-friendly, offering added protection against leaks. They also help to reduce noise and make for a slightly softer 'feel'.

Regular (above) and rolled (below) toneholes (Keilwerth).

Posts

The posts that hold the key system in place are soldered onto the body either individually (*post construction*), or, more commonly, in groups, by means of metal strips (*rib* or *ribbed construction*). The latter makes the instrument a bit sturdier. As the ribs may constrict the sound and resonance of the instrument a bit, some makers have reduced their size and weight. Other companies offer instruments with a partial ribbed construction.

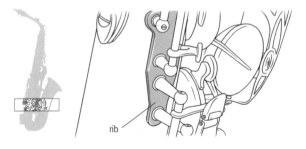

rib

Saxophone with ribbed construction.

Detachable bell

Another detail: Many saxophones feature a detachable bell, and on some the bow can be removed too. This offers easy access for removing dents, for instance.

THE KEY SYSTEM

Over the years, the key system has undergone lots of improvements. Modern saxophones are easier to play, key shapes have been adapted for a more comfortable feel, extra keys have been added while others disappeared, and adjustable side and palm keys have been introduced.

Nineteen

The very first saxes had nineteen keys. More and more were added, as the illustration on page 28 shows. Other keys disappeared over the years. Most modern saxes have twenty-four or twenty-five keys, the extra one being the high F♯.

High F♯

The *high F♯ key* makes playing this high note a little easier. This key, introduced in the 1960s, is now a standard item on most but the cheaper instruments, and some companies offer it as an option. Before you spend the extra money, note that you'll only get around to those high notes once you've been playing for quite some time.

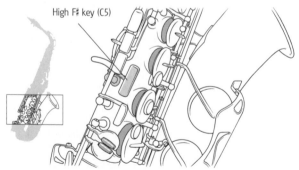

High F♯ key (C5)

The high F♯ key. The tonehole is located higher up (see next page).

High F♯, no key

Some saxophonists prefer horns without the high F♯ key, as they feel it affects the instrument's timbre. Besides, most good players can play this note without the extra key. The

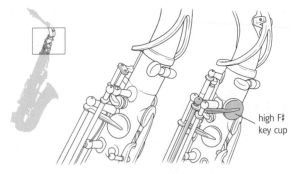

high F#
key cup

A sax without (left), and one with a high F# (right).

same goes for high G, a note for which some soprano saxes have an extra key.

Low A

An extra key found on most modern baritones is *low A*. To produce this note *low A baritones* are slightly longer than the traditional baris. Note that 'low A' only refers to the horn's lowest note, and not to its tuning: Low A baritones are still B♭ instruments!

Automatic octave key

Occasionally, catalogs promote saxophones by extolling their *automatic octave key*. Sounds impressive, but this has been a standard item since the 1930s. When you press the octave key, the mechanism 'automatically' determines which of the two octave vents should be opened. The lower octave vent opens for the lower notes of the upper register (D through G♯). On higher notes the upper octave vent opens, and the first one closes automatically. Before, saxes had a separate key for each octave vent.

Automatic G♯

The *automatic G♯* or *articulated G♯*, introduced on expensive instruments in the 1930s, has also become pretty much a standard feature. It opens the G♯ key when you are using the low C♯, B, or B♭ key (left little finger), making it easier to alternate between any of these notes and G♯. However, the system has one drawback: Your little finger has to work harder because it has to operate so many keys simultaneously. That's why some saxes have the option of disengaging it.

Non-sticking G♯

The G♯ key cup tends to stick rather easily. To make sure it opens every time it needs to, saxophones have features with names like 'G♯ Pad Cup Lifting Mechanism' or 'Spring-Controlled G♯.'

Articulated C♯

If you play a low B or low B♭, your left little finger can easily get hung up on the C♯ key. The result? C♯, instead of the intended notes. Most saxes therefore have a small rod that closes the C♯ key as soon as you use the low B or B♭ key. This *articulated C♯* ensures that you get the note you want.

Tilting keys

Most professional and some of the more affordable saxes feature *tilting little finger keys*. When you play the C♯ key, for example, the B♭ key tilts toward it, making shifts between these notes a lot easier. This is especially useful for certain technical passages.

Additional keys

Occasionally, saxophones have other special keys. For example, there are saxophones with an extra key that operates a second vent hole on the neck, making the high harmonics easier to play. Other extra keys are 'automatic,' such as special keys that correct the pitch of certain notes by closing or opening one or more vents.

Lingo

Most of the features that may help you select an instrument have been included on these pages. However, when reading catalogs and brochures, you're bound to come across many more technical terms and other saxophone lingo, such as *floating-* or *rocker-type mechanisms*. Usually, these terms do not refer to things that might influence the way the instrument plays or sounds in any significant way.

Power-forged keys

Sometimes you find saxophones advertised as having *power-forged* keys – but this is a standard item on pretty much every sax: It means the keys are shaped by pressure, when the metal is cold, rather than cast.

Double key arms

To enhance their stability and help prevent damage and misaligned keys, some manufacturers use double key arms for the pad cups of the large bell keys (low C and lower).

ERGONOMICS

Every alto sax is the same size. All tenors are the same size too – and so on. However, it is likely that one make or series suits you better than another. Even the exact location of the hanger loop may be of influence, for example.

Sit down

Though standing up is often considered the best way to play a wind instrument, as this position gives you better air stream control, many musicians play sitting down – so try out a horn that way too.

Side and palm keys

Check the position of the side and palm keys. If they sit high, and you have small hands, you may find them difficult to reach, or you may open them accidentally. A compact design may be easier to play – even if you have bigger hands.

Oversized and contoured

Another way to improve fingering ease and the playing comfort of the instrument is to use oversized keys and levers, for instance for high F♯ and the side F♯ key, or sculptured (contoured, concave, finger fitting…) spatula keys, pearls, or palm keys.

Another style

Some companies do a lot of design research themselves; others rely on well-established designs. *French style keys*, for instance, are keys that are modeled after a design of the French Selmer saxophones. When trying out saxophones, some models may feel kind of weird at first, due to differently shaped keys – but you get used to another key design pretty quickly.

Adjustable keys

To make the instrument fit your hands and your style of playing, most better saxophones come with a number of

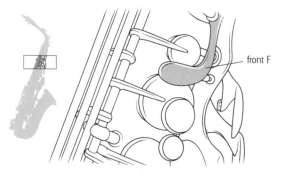

Sax with a spatula key for the front F.

adjustable keys – either as a standard feature, or as an option. Examples are G♯, high F, E, D, and some of the little finger and palm keys.

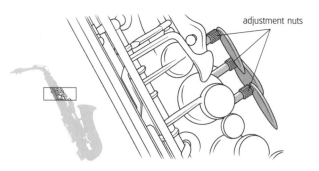

Adjustable palm keys (Keilwerth).

Risers and extensions
Alternatively, a saxophone technician can adjust your instrument to your liking by reshaping keys or by replacing some of the bumpers with thinner or thicker ones. Should the side or palm keys be too low, a set of *key risers* can make them more accessible. These risers can easily be self-installed. For other keys, various types of key extensions are available, and some keys can be built up with cork or epoxy, for example.

Adjustable thumb hooks
Most thumb hooks can be adjusted both sideways and up and down. If not the case with your instrument, you can usually have its thumb hook replaced by an adjustable one.

Plastic or metal

Thumb hooks come in plastic and metal. Some players find the plastic ones more comfortable, and plastic hooks can't discolor or cause skin rash. If a metal hook bothers you, you can slide a soft (imitation) rubber *thumb saver* over it.

Thumb hooks and sound

Conversely, some sensitive players replace their thumb hooks by special metal versions that are claimed to improve the sound of the horn, enhancing its resonance and helping to produce a bigger and more brilliant sound. Sound-enhancing metal replacement thumb rests are also available.

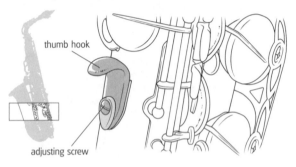

thumb hook

adjusting screw

Adjustable thumb hook.

SPRINGS AND ADJUSTMENT

When play-testing saxophones, you'll notice that some instruments play easier or faster than others – each horn has a different *action*, to use the lingo. A horn's action depends on the quality of the keywork, and its adjustment.

Heavy or light

On a well-adjusted instrument, the springs are set to give all keys the same resistance. If the springs are adjusted too lightly, you may find that you can't really feel what you're doing, or that the keys become sluggish and don't return as quickly as they should. Keys that require too much pressure make you work too hard and slow you down.

Key height

Key height should be properly adjusted as well. Key cups that open too far will slow you down and affect intonation for the worse (see page 49). Adjusting action and key heights are jobs for a specialized technician.

Sticking and bouncing

The keys should return quickly and smoothly to their resting positions when you release them: They're not supposed to stick, bounce, or rattle. You can test this by lightly depressing each and every key cup, and quickly sliding your finger off it sideways. Clattering keys can be caused by faulty adjustment too, and on used instruments missing felts or corks may be the culprit. Sticking keys can also be caused by sticky pads (see page 98).

Springs

Most saxophones come with standard steel needle springs. Their blue or black hue is caused by a tempering treatment that gives the springs their required elasticity. The springs for the larger closed key cups (low C♯ and D♯) should be strong enough to make the pads seal the toneholes.

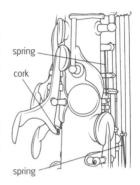

spring
cork
spring

PADS

The majority of saxophones have leather pads, consisting of a felt disc covered with a thin layer of sheep, goat, or baby goat (kid) leather. To seal the toneholes properly, the

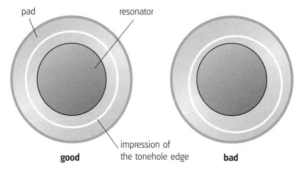

pad   resonator

good   impression of   bad
        the tonehole edge

The impression of the collar of the tonehole must be exactly in the middle of the pad.

pads must be exactly centered over the holes. You can check this by looking at the impression of the tonehole's edge in the pad.

Resonators

Resonators, the small discs in the middle of each pad, make the instrument sound a bit more direct and responsive, enhancing its brightness, cutting power, and projection. That's why some call them *tone boosters*. To mellow down an overly bright horn, you may consider using plastic resonators rather than the regular metal ones. Pads without resonators will make most saxophones sound lifeless and dull.

Why leather?

Even though most players still prefer them, the traditional leather pads have quite some disadvantages: They require a lot of maintenance, and even then they don't last, mainly due to the fact that leather doesn't like to get wet and dry out repeatedly.

Non-leather pads

Non-leather pads, made of synthetic materials or rubber compounds, are insensitive to changes in humidity and easily outlast leather pads. Over the years they have been continuously improved, and their acceptance has grown accordingly.

(Dis)advantages

Synthetic pads are often said to improve sealing and thus enhance resonance and response; they don't stick the way leather pads do; and they require less maintenance. On the other hand, they're usually more expensive than leather ones; they often require the toneholes of the instrument to be perfectly leveled; and some players just don't like the way they make their horn sound, play, or both.

Faster

Some synthetic pad designs even allow for replacing the traditional key cups on the lowest toneholes by lightweight metal discs with built-in pads. The resulting weight reduction means that less spring tension is needed, which adds up to an even faster action.

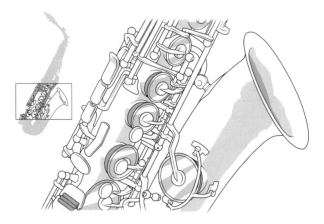

A saxophone with lightweight metal discs, rather than the traditional
key cups (TopTone Systems).

Pop

Pads that properly seal their toneholes make a resonant,
'pop'-like sound when closing the relevant key. However, a
series of solid pops does not guarantee that a horn is
leak-free. See page 55 for tips on how to locate leaks.

PLAY-TESTING

To judge the sound and intonation of a saxophone, you
need to be able to play pretty well. If you don't (yet...), take
a good saxophonist with you to try out the tips and tricks
on the following pages, or go to a store that employs one.

Somebody else

If someone else plays a couple of instruments for you,
they'll never sound the same as if you were to play them
yourself – but you will be able to hear the differences
between the instruments. A tip: Even if you do play
yourself, ask somebody else to play for you just to hear
how the various horns sound from a distance. You'll find
that you hear things you didn't hear before. Alternatively,
you can point the instruments at a wall when you play, so
that their sound is reflected back to you. This also helps
when checking their intonation.

The mouthpiece

To play-test horns, always use one mouthpiece (preferably

your own) and reed. If not, you'll be comparing mouth-pieces as much as saxophones. Ultimately, however, the saxophone of your choice may perform better with another mouthpiece and reed combination.

Two tests in advance

There are two tests that allow you to quickly find out if a sax plays well enough to judge it.

- Play the instrument using **as little air** pressure as possible, and press the keys as lightly as you can. If you need to blow harder or squeeze the keys to get a note out, something is probably wrong.
- Play a B, pressing key 1 with your left index finger. Then **go down the scale**, softly, note by note, until you reach low Bb. The lowest notes are the trickiest ones. If the sax is leaking even a tiny bit, you'll have trouble getting them to speak.

IN TUNE

On a saxophone you need to use your embouchure and air stream control to determine the exact pitch of the notes you play. This takes some time to learn, but you simply have to: A saxophone is never perfectly in tune by itself.

Why not?

Why not? A saxophone could only be made to play every note perfectly in tune if it had an octave vent for each note – and there's just no room for that. Also, the positions of all toneholes are interrelated, which makes it impossible to make them all perfectly right. For example, high C♯ always sounds a bit sharp. This can be corrected by enlarging one or more toneholes, or by moving them down the tube just a bit – but that would make other notes sound flat.

Better intonation

The better in tune the sax is to begin with, the less you'll need to adjust the notes. In other words, the better a saxophone's *intonation*, the easier it will be to play in tune.

Smaller is harder

The smaller the instrument, the more critical the placement and the exact size of the toneholes are: A thousandth of an inch has more effect on a soprano than on a baritone. That's why sopranos are harder to make (and play) in tune than larger horns.

Tuning, leaks, and key openings
The intonation of a sax can be judged only if it has been tuned (see page 85), if key heights have been properly adjusted (key openings that are too large will make notes flat, and vice versa), and if there are no leaking pads. An electronic tuner may be very helpful for the following tests.

Open C♯
One test is to go from open C♯ (no keys depressed) to the D above that note. This C♯ is always a bit flat, while low D is often a tad sharp.

Larger intervals
Also play larger intervals, such as fifths (C–G, D–A, and so on) and octaves (C–C, D–D; *i.e.*, notes with and without the octave key) and check whether they sound in tune with one another – or rather, how easily you can play them in tune. For example, open C♯ being a little flat, and high C♯ a bit sharp, you will always have to adjust those pitches with your embouchure.

Harmonic series
For advanced players only: You can play a whole range of notes without moving from one fingering position, but using your air stream and embouchure only. You are then playing the *harmonic series* or the *harmonics* of the note you're fingering.
When you finger low B♭, the first harmonic is the B♭ an octave higher, the second is the F above that, then the next B♭ and the D follow, and so on. These harmonics should be in tune with one another.

Best buy
The less in tune a sax plays, the better you have to play to make it sound acceptable. That's why beginners are better off buying a sax that plays in tune easily, rather than one that sounds great but has poor intonation. Horns that do both well are usually more expensive…

LISTENING TIPS

Comparing instruments' sounds or timbres isn't easy – but the more often you do it, the more you'll hear. And the better you can play, the better you'll be able to appreciate the subtle timbre differences between horns. Here are some tips that can be helpful, followed by some remarks on what to listen for.

Briefly at first

To make an initial selection of horns that you like, play them only briefly. Play something simple, otherwise you'll be concentrating more on playing than on listening. Scales, for instance, nice and slowly. If there's one sax that stands out from the rest at this stage, that'll often be the one you end up buying.

Two by two

Once you've found a number of instruments that you really like, compare them two by two or three by three. Choose the best one and replace the one you like least with another horn. Again choose the best one, and so on.

A little longer

In order to choose the very best horn from the two or three that remain, you may want to play each one a little longer so that you get to know them better. A tip: Even after just fifteen minutes of playing it gets harder to hear the differences. Take a break, or come back a day or two later.

With your ears alone

Also try listening to these horns without looking to see which one you're playing: Use your ears only, without being influenced by prices, brand names, looks, or anything else. If the one that sounds best and plays best turns out to be the cheapest one, that's a bonus. Unless you particularly wanted a more expensive one, of course…

Sheet music

If you don't know any music by heart, take sheet music with you when you go to choose a new horn. The better you know a piece, the less you will be thinking about the notes, and the better you can concentrate on the instrument.

No idea

If you have no idea where to start when you walk into a store, ask for two horns with distinctively different timbres – one with a notably dark tone and another that sounds particularly bright, for example. Decide what you like best and go on from there. Another tip: Play both the cheapest and the most expensive instrument available. Knowing the extremes can often help you to determine where you want to go.

Your own horn

If you already own a saxophone, take it with you when you go out to buy a new one. That makes it easier to hear just how different instruments sound. On the other hand: You may be so used to your own instrument that it may seem to sound better or more in tune than other horns – even compared to more expensive ones.

Different words

When two people listen to the same saxophone, they often use very different words to describe what they hear. What one considers shrill and thin (and so not attractive), another may consider bright or brilliant (and so not unattractive). And what one describes as dark and velvety, another may think dull or stuffy. Similarly, what one finds dark, another may find bright... It all depends on what you like, and on the words you use to describe it.

Character

What sounds good and what doesn't also depends on the kind of music you play. If you play classical music, you're probably looking for a more controlled and intimate sound than if you play jazz. And jazz players may want a more expressive sound, while Latin musicians may look for something brighter and more focused. Some saxophones allow you to play different styles and produce a wide range of tonal colors easier than other, less versatile instruments.

Loud and soft

To judge the instruments, play them both loudly and softly throughout their entire range, and do so while playing each note separately, as well as joined together (*legato*).

Low and high

Low notes should sound big and fat, even at low volumes. The highest notes should sound bright and clear, without getting too shrill or edgy, even when playing them loud.

Tight and quick

When playing very loud, you should still be able to produce a focused, tight sound, without any notes breaking up – unless you want them to. Also play as softly as you can, and listen to hear if every note, from high to low, responds quickly and easily.

A gradual change

Every horn sounds bigger, fuller, or fatter in its low register. In the high register, the tone will be thinner and tighter. When you play the instrument from low to high, that change should occur gradually. A critical spot is the jump between registers, from open C♯ to D – a half-step that involves closing a large number of keys.

Preferences

Some players do prefer horns that have quite a big contrast between the higher and lower ranges; others – mainly classical players – prefer a more even-sounding instrument.

Your sound

As a final note: Saxophonists differ in sound much more than saxophones do. The saxophone that 'sounds best' to you, is probably the instrument that does most justice to your sound, and that allows your sound to come out easily.

SECONDHAND INSTRUMENTS

If you're thinking of purchasing a used instrument, there are a few additional things you need to pay attention to. Number one: It's always advisable to have an expert appraise a used horn before you decide to buy it. A few special tips on buying vintage or classic instruments can be found at the end of this chapter.

The lacquer

The lacquer may have started to wear off, and on old horns there are various spots where it may have disappeared completely – especially where the instrument rubs against the player's hands and clothes. You may not like the looks, but worn-off lacquer will not influence the sound to any noticeable degree.

Newly lacquered

Older saxes sporting a shiny lacquer finish all over the instrument haven't been played very much, or they've been relacquered. Relacquering involves removing the original lacquer, a process which usually takes away some of the body's metal as well. The latter will influence the instrument's sound, and it may also result in an ill-fitting, wobbling key system. If too much lacquer has been applied to the horn, the sound will be muffled. This doesn't mean, however, that every relacquered sax is a bad one.

Silver or nickel, gold or lacquer

It's not hard to spot the difference between (expensive) silver-plated or (inexpensive) nickel-plated horns: Nickel chips and turns grayish, while silver wears down gradually and turns blue or black where polishing cloths can't reach it. Spotting the difference between gold-lacquered and (rare) gold-plated horns often requires a specialist's eye.

Dents

Check the body, bell, and neck for dents. The further down the instrument, the less effect a dent will have. Conversely, even a tiny dent in the neck can impair a horn's intonation and timbre. Dents in the body can dislocate the key system, hindering the movement of certain keys. They can also alter the rigidity of the body, which may influence the tone.

Besides their severity, the cost of removing dents depends on how hard it is to reach them (a removable bell helps; see page 39). Used horns can also suffer from cracks or split soldering seams, but finding them usually requires an expert.

The neck

Check the neck's shape too, especially when you're looking at a tenor or a baritone. These instruments may suffer from necks that have been bent down a little: Many players inadvertently exert a downward pressure on the neck when putting on the mouthpiece. This may result in one or more poorly responding notes, among other problems.

The right neck

Of course, the neck should fit the saxophone in every sense (see page 37). Note that a different finish doesn't always mean that the neck doesn't belong to the instrument (see page 33).

Rods and keys   Tipcode SAX-012

Carefully check the key system. Worn-out key pearls can be easily replaced. If the instrument has a feather-light action, chances are that the springs need to be adjusted or replaced. A very light action may also be the result of a lot of play or wobble. Try the rods for play: They should not be able to move back and forth or sideways. Similarly, keys and key cups should only move up and down. Check the rollers between the little finger keys as well; they should only roll and not move sideways. Play may cause leaks, as the key system will fail to properly seal the toneholes. Play also slows down the action; it's a source of squeaks and rattles, and it always gets worse.

Bent rods

Check the rods to see if they're straight. Bend rods obstruct the action. The larger the horn, the longer its rods, the more vulnerable it is. Larger horns are more susceptible to dents too, because of their size.

Rust and solder

Look for rust at the ends of rods and on screws. Rusty parts can drastically slow down the mechanism. Globs of solder can be a sign that the instrument has been sloppily repaired. This doesn't necessarily indicate an ineffective repair, but it does reduce the instrument's value.

A snug fit

To make the mouthpiece fit snugly, the *neck cork* shouldn't be overcompressed or falling apart. If it is, you can't play-test the instrument unless you fix it temporarily with thread or paper (see page 87). The neck cork can easily be replaced. Also check to see that the neck tenon easily fits its receiver, and that there's no play in the joint. If there is, air will escape, affecting both intonation and response.

Leaking pads

The pads should be smooth and soft. Locating a leaking pad is not as simple as it may seem. If, for instance, the low C doesn't respond well, it doesn't necessarily follow that the C key is the culprit – the leak could occur at a higher pad too. Slide a piece of paper under the suspect pads, and close them gently with the relevant keys. (For closed keys, rely on the spring to keep them closed.) If you don't feel any resistance when pulling the paper away, you've probably found your leak. Sax technicians check for leaks with a special *leak light* that is inserted in the instrument. Where light leaks out, air will too. A bent neck or a leaking neck/body connection may also be the culprit.

Too high, too low

Today most bands and orchestras tune to A=440 (see page 85), and saxophones are designed to play at that pitch. You may find older horns, however, that were built to be tuned slightly higher or lower. You can learn how to play on such an instrument, but you won't be able to play it in a band that tunes to A=440. (You may be able to tune to that pitch, but by then your mouthpiece will be so far in or out that the intonation of your instrument will be off completely; again, see page 85.) Another disadvantage is that you'll have to adjust both your intonation and your hearing when you change to a modern horn later on.

HP, LP

Saxes with a higher standard tuning can be identified by the abbreviation HP (high pitch) or by the indication A=451 or A=902, for example. Horns with a lower tuning have a number below 440 or 880, and they're often marked LP (low pitch). These indications are usually located near the serial number, below the thumb hook or on the bell. You can also tell an instrument with a deviant pitch by its length: HP instruments are about an inch shorter than saxes with standard tuning; low-pitched ones are about an inch taller.

Smell

If you go out to try an older used sax and a terrible smell comes wafting out of the case, you are looking at a poorly-maintained instrument, or at an instrument that hasn't been used in a long, long time. Don't worry: If the instrument is worth it, it can be completely restored (see page 101).

VINTAGE SAXOPHONES

Many professional jazz players prefer classic or vintage saxophones, which are often said to sound darker and fatter than today's horns, and to offer a bigger dynamic range. Some examples are listed in Chapter 14, *Brands*.

Not all the same

Not every vintage sax is a good one. For one thing, when horns were still made by hand, the differences between 'identical' instruments were greater than they are today. One vintage horn of a reputable type and year, therefore, may not be as good as the other.

A good player

Saxophonists who favor vintage horns often love their tonal range, and the fact that they can color the timbre to a large extent. Of course you need to be able to truly play the instrument if you want to harness and control its flexibility, and to play the horn in tune: Most vintage instruments are not known for their great intonation. Also, they require a better air stream control and breath support.

Heavier action

In the old days, much less was done to create ergonomic designs. One example? Today's octave key, shaped in a sort of crescent around the thumb rest, is a lot easier to play

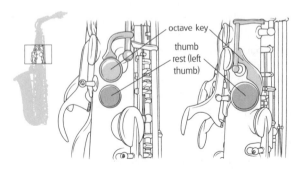

Left: Round octave key on a 1927 Buescher Truetone.
Right: A modern octave key. The palm keys are also different.

than the old-fashioned button key. Old altos are less of a problem than vintage tenors or baris, as their keys are slightly closer together and you're moving less metal.

Special keys
Old saxes may have keys that new ones don't. An example is the G♯ trill key, designed to play trills between G and G♯ with your right middle finger. It was used on certain German and American saxes made before 1940, as was a special key to trill between D and D♯.

Vintage mouthpieces
The older a horn is, the harder it will be to find it a matching mouthpiece. Modern mouthpieces usually don't work well with the vintage saxes. First of all, they don't make them sound like vintage saxes. Also, certain notes may not respond well, and the entire instrument can sound out of balance or out of tune. Vintage mouthpieces are usually shorter and may have extremely round chambers, rather than the modern, 'straight' type of chamber, as you can see below.

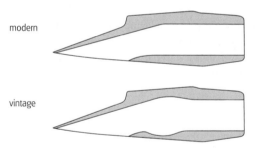

modern

vintage

Vintage mouthpieces (below) often have a large, round chamber.

Many years
And finally: If you find yourself a good vintage horn and take good care of it, it will retain its value for many years – and it may even increase. On the other hand, musical instruments are usually not the best investments if you want to enlarge your capital.

7. MOUTHPIECES AND LIGATURES

Next to the reed, the mouthpiece is the most important part of your instrument. A well-chosen mouthpiece allows you to play everything you want to play as effortlessly as possible. The ligature plays a role too, both in the sound and the playability of your saxophone.

For beginners, the best mouthpiece is one that allows you to play as easily as possible. If you've been playing longer, you'll try to find a mouthpiece that allows you to effortlessly do everything you want to – playing loud and soft, low and high, short and long notes, with a fast response and the resistance and timbre you're looking for. Usually, that won't be the same mouthpiece as the one you started out on.

A good fit
Just like a pair of shoes, a mouthpiece has to be a perfect fit. What fits you, when it comes to mouthpieces, is determined by your technique, your embouchure, and, eventually, the sound you're looking for.

How it works
The vibration of the reed causes the air inside the mouthpiece to vibrate. The resulting sound has a lot to do with the design of the mouthpiece. An example? Your voice sounds different in a restroom than it does in the average living room. A mouthpiece has a 'room' too: the *chamber*. A different chamber will make for a different sound.

The main parts
These are the main elements of a mouthpiece:

- The *tip opening* is the space between the tip of the reed and the tip of the mouthpiece.
- The *facing length* or *lay* is the distance from the tip opening to where the reed first touches the mouthpiece.
- The *window* is the opening under the reed. Look through the window, and you'll see the chamber.
- The neck enters the mouthpiece at the *bore* or *barrel*.

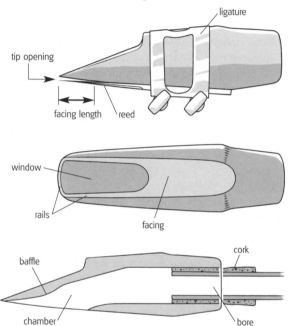

A mouthpiece shown from the side, from below, and in cross-section.

Dimensions or words?

Mouthpiece brochures usually tell you the exact sizes of the tip opening and facing length of each mouthpiece. On their own, these figures don't tell you too much, though: A mouthpiece has many more dimensions that affect its performance. So it's often more useful to read what a brochure says about the sound you can expect from a certain mouthpiece, and about the style of music for which it has been designed. An intimate, controlled sound for classical music. Or a sound that blends well, for ensemble playing. Or lots of volume and projection for wind bands that play outdoors, or great flexibility and expressiveness for jazz.

Open or close

Sax players talk about *open* or *close* mouthpieces. An open mouthpiece, with a large tip opening, makes for a bigger sound. This requires a good embouchure and well-developed breath control. A close mouthpiece, with a small tip opening, plays more easily, and creates a less open, more controlled type of sound.

Beginners

Most beginners start with a medium-close mouthpiece. Well-designed beginner's mouthpieces help you to play with little effort and to learn to voice the notes accurately. Budget saxophones don't always come with a mouthpiece that qualifies as 'good,' however, and it often pays off to change it for one that does – even at a higher price.

Reed-friendly

A good beginner's mouthpiece is also reed-friendly: Most reeds work well on them.

Big opening

Not every mouthpiece/reed combination that plays easily is a good choice for beginners. For example, you may find 'student' mouthpieces with a large tip opening and a soft reed, which play very easily. However, this combination makes it hard to voice the notes and to develop a good sound.

Hundreds

Once you've been playing for a couple of years, you can enhance your sound with a professional mouthpiece – and there are literally hundreds to choose from. Depending on how well you play, what and how you play, and what you're looking for, you can easily make a basic selection of a handful of mouthpieces, or have a salesperson make a pre-selection for you.

Comparing

Comparing mouthpieces is not very different from comparing saxophones (see pages 50–52). Always try mouthpieces on your own instrument, as they are very likely to behave differently on another horn. One extra tip: You may want to use a mouthpiece disinfectant to prevent rashes and other symptoms.

The price tag

The price can also be a deciding factor in your choice. There are decent beginners' mouthpieces that sell for less than fifty dollars, but be prepared to pay up to a hundred or more. Professionals sometimes spend two to three hundred dollars and up for special designs.

THE DIFFERENCES

How a mouthpiece plays and sounds depends on the tip opening, the length and curvature of the facing, the size and shape of the chamber, and much else besides.

Different ideas

Almost every mouthpiece company seems to have its own ideas when it comes to mouthpiece classifications, and to how 'open' and 'close' mouthpieces relate to one another. For example, with some brands the facing length increases proportionately with the tip opening. Other makers offer two or three facing lengths, combined with a dozen different tip openings – and so on.

Corresponding types

The way makers name their mouthpieces isn't very unambiguous either. An example? Most brands have an alto mouthpiece with a tip opening of $70/1000$" (1.8 mm). Dukoff calls it a D5, Otto Link a 5*, Lawton a 6, Vandoren an A27, and Selmer a C*... Only a few brands call it a 70 – the number that directly refers to the actual size of the tip opening.

Tables

Fortunately, to make your quest a bit easier, there are tables listing the characteristics of similar mouthpieces by different brands side by side. You can find them on the Internet and in music stores.

A higher number

One of the few consistencies in classifying mouthpieces is that a higher number or letter generally indicates a more open mouthpiece, within one make or series – so a 6 of one brand may still be more open than an 8 of another company.

Asterisk

An asterisk is often used to indicate in-between sizes: A 5* ('five star') is between a 5 and a 6. Usually an asterisk refers to a larger tip opening, which is sometimes combined with a larger facing.

Same opening, different sound

With mouthpieces, you can't simply line up the variables alongside one another and compare. After all, two mouthpieces with identical tip openings may be radically different, due to their respective chambers, facings, baffles, and so on. With that in mind, consider the following tips as a general guide.

TIP OPENING

Differences between tip openings are quite large: For one type of sax, the largest opening is more than twice (!) as big as the smallest.

Tip openings for alto and tenor mouthpieces.

	most commonly used	very small	very large
alto	70–100 (1.8–2.5mm)	50 (1.3mm)	125 (3.2mm)
tenor	90–120 (2–3mm)	55 (1.4mm)	145 (3.7mm)

A mouthpiece with a smaller tip opening:

- produces a focused, 'smaller,' tighter sound;
- is easier to control;
- makes the instrument respond faster and speak easier;
- is more suitable for classical music and for concert bands;
- produces less volume and is easier to play softly;
- requires a harder reed.

A mouthpiece with a larger tip opening:

- produces a larger, more open and muscular sound, with more body;
- is harder to control (pitch, for one thing) and requires a better player;
- is more suitable for jazz, rock, Latin, and similar styles;
- produces more volume and is harder to play softly;
- offers more possibilities for controlling the sound and the intonation;
- asks for a softer reed.

A beginner?

For beginners, a mouthpiece with a relatively small to medium tip opening and a medium reed is often the best choice. The combination of a small tip opening and a hard reed isn't easy to play for a beginner. Combining a large tip opening with a soft reed will easily result in an unsteady sound.

The hardest combination

A large tip opening with a hard reed is one of the hardest combinations to play on. It also produces the biggest sound, which is why you mainly find it on the horns of pro musicians in jazz, rock, and similar styles.

Inches and millimeters

Tip openings are usually stated in thousandths of an inch, so 70 equals 70/1000" or .0070. If you want to convert this to millimeters, multiply by 0.0254 (0.0254 x 70 = 1.8 mm).

THE FACING

A larger tip opening means the reed has to travel over a larger distance, which means that a larger part of the reed has to be able to vibrate. A longer facing or *lay* allows it that freedom.

Curvature and facing

At least as important as its length is the curvature of the facing, though brochures tell you next to nothing about that. The main reason is that it is not easy to describe how 'curved' a facing is.

A length for each opening

Mouthpieces are usually classified by their tip opening, and most manufacturers have a certain facing length for each tip opening they offer. In other words: The facing length often comes with the tip opening.

A longer facing

Other makers offer mouthpieces with a choice of facing lengths for each tip opening. Many saxophonists feel that a longer facing adds more bottom or core to the sound, and that it makes a large tip opening easier to control. If it gets too long, however, it can render the sound dull and lifeless. In other words: A longer facing isn't always the solution for a weak tone.

The measurements

The facings of alto mouthpieces vary between approximately .600" (15 mm; very short) and .1000" (25 mm; very long). On tenor mouthpieces they roughly range between .670" (17 mm) and 1.175" (30 mm). Facing lengths are usually stated in tenths of an inch. To get millimeters, multiply by 25.4.

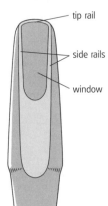

tip rail

side rails

window

The rails

The edges or *rails* of the mouthpiece are also part of the facing. If the *side rails* are not exactly the same shape and thickness, the mouthpiece will be out of balance. As a result, you may get squeaks, or your instrument may have a poor response or a shrill sound.

Thick rails, fat sound

The thickness of the side rails and the *tip rail* also affect the tone. If you're an advanced player, narrow rails will help you produce a bright, clear, crisp sound. For less experienced musicians such rails increase the risk of squeaks and an edgy, shrill tone. Thicker rails will get you a less brilliant, darker, fatter sound, and they make playing softly a little easier. Cheap mouthpieces generally have thicker rails – not so much for their tonal or playing characteristics, but because they are easier to produce.

Smooth

The rails should always be perfectly smooth. The tip rail should have the same shape as the tip of the reed, and the side rails should have the same thickness and curvature left and right. This is often one of the problem areas for cheap plastic mouthpieces.

CHAMBERS AND BAFFLES

Many brands offer a choice of chamber sizes – another

important variable. At least as important is whether the mouthpiece has a baffle.

Chambers
A larger chamber generally gives a darker, warmer, rounder, mellower sound, which blends well. It also makes for a more versatile mouthpiece that allows you more control over your timbre. With a smaller chamber you basically get a 'smaller,' more focused, tighter, edgier type of sound with the ability to cut through the music. High notes speak easier; low notes a little harder.

Just the chamber
Some companies offer series of mouthpieces that differ in chamber size only, in order to allow you to change your sound without having to adapt your embouchure to another tip opening or facing.

The baffle
The effect of a baffle can be compared to what happens if you squeeze the end of a garden hose, producing a more forceful, focused water jet: A mouthpiece with a baffle makes your sound more forceful and focused, with a brighter and edgier timbre. The higher the baffle, the more it will funnel your air stream and the stronger its effect will be. A mouthpiece with very little or no baffle helps to produce a smoother and warmer, more controllable and ensemble-oriented sound.

Who's using what
Of course, there's a relationship between baffle and chamber size: The larger the baffle, the smaller the chamber becomes. As you may have figured out from the above, classical players usually use mouthpieces with larger

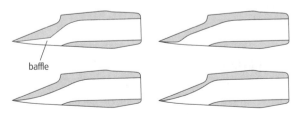

Various baffles (Vandoren).

chambers and no baffles, while saxophonists who need a bright, penetrating sound will usually go for small chambers and large baffles.

Self-adhesive or adjustable

If you want to experiment with the effect of a baffle, get yourself a set of self-adhesive baffles. They won't do the same as a baffle that was carefully designed within the context of the mouthpiece, but you'll get the idea. Also, there are mouthpieces with an adjustable baffle, which allows you to alter your sound to meet different room acoustics or musical situations – a brighter sound for a 'deader' sounding room or solo work, for example, or a smoother tone for ensemble playing.

Throat

If you look through the barrel of a mouthpiece, at the opposite end from the tip, you'll see the shape of the *throat*. The larger the throat, the darker, smoother, and warmer the sound will be. A smaller throat makes for a brighter, edgier type of sound.

Free blowing

The throat also helps determine the playing resistance of the mouthpiece. Some saxophonists prefer a very free-blowing mouthpiece, while others like to feel some resistance – a choice that may have to do with your lung capacity as well.

Round or square

Throats may be round, square, or square with rounded corners. The influence of this shape can't be considered separately from the other dimensions of the mouthpiece – which helps explain why some experts consider a round model ideal for unrestricted, free air flow, while others make the same claim for square ones...

MATERIALS

Most mouthpieces are made of either hard rubber or metal. Hard rubber, also known as *ebonite*, is the most common material for classical and all-round mouthpieces. Metal mouthpieces are more often used by advanced jazz and rock musicians. However, there are also edgy-sounding hard rubber mouthpieces, just as there are metal mouthpieces for classical saxophonists.

Size over matter

This shows that the material is not the most critical factor in affecting the instrument's sound. Though most mouthpiece makers choose metal for their 'bright and powerful' designs, the dimensions of the mouthpiece play a greater role in producing that timbre. It follows that you can't simply say that bronze mouthpieces sound darker than steel ones, for instance.

Size difference

Playing a metal mouthpiece feels very different from playing a rubber one. Not only because metal just 'feels' different, but also because metal mouthpieces have smaller outer dimensions than hard rubber ones. Some players like this, others don't. Soundwise, the fact that your mouth is less open when using a metal mouthpiece may contribute to the slightly more focused, tighter sound these mouthpieces are known for.

Noisy

Finally, playing a metal mouthpiece may produce unwanted noise due to moisture that collects inside: Your breath easily condenses on this material, especially – but not only – when it's cold. This is one more reason that you hardly ever see metal mouthpieces used by classical musicians.

Plastic

Good plastic mouthpieces can be made, but this material is typically used for the cheapest models, as it allows for easy and fast production. Low-budget saxophones often come with plastic mouthpieces. Note that there are professional synthetic mouthpieces as well, made of polycarbonate, for example.

Other materials

Some manufacturers use other materials, such as a mix of graphite and synthetics, and a few even make wood, crystal, or ceramic mouthpieces. Some companies sell mouthpieces in various colors.

Bite plate

The vibration of a metal mouthpiece is rather strong. To reduce the effect that these vibrations have on your upper teeth, most metal mouthpieces have a hard rubber *bite plate*.

Mouthpiece cushions

Is the vibration still too much? Then use one or two *mouthpiece cushions*. These soft, self-adhesive patches are used on other types of mouthpieces as well, for example to prevent teeth marks on ebonite or plastic models. Mouthpiece cushions also enhance a stable embouchure by helping you keep your mouthpiece from sliding to different positions in your mouth. They come separately or in sets, and in different hardnesses and thicknesses. Some brands adhere better than others. Finding the cushions that work best for you is a matter of trial and error, but they're not expensive.

A different sound?

Many saxophonists feel that using mouthpiece cushions alters your sound. This is mainly because you perceive your sound differently, as the cushion muffles the vibrations that pass on through your teeth and skull. Someone else, in other words, won't hear the difference.

MOUTHPIECE BUYING TIPS

- If your sax doesn't play well, **have it checked** before trying to solve the problem by buying a new mouthpiece. Also make sure the problem is not your choice of reeds – or your playing.
- Always keep your embouchure and level of development in mind when buying a mouthpiece, and try to avoid buying **one you can't handle** because of a tip opening, facing, baffle, or chamber that's either too large or too small.
- If you **play other woodwinds** as well, this may influence your choice: If the best saxophone mouthpiece you can find bothers you when changing to and from the clarinet, for example, you may have to decide to buy another one.
- Choosing the perfect mouthpiece quickly will always be difficult: You only really get to know a new mouthpiece after **a few weeks' playing**.

- A tuning line on the neck cork (see page 87) won't be of much use when play-testing mouthpieces, as they can differ in length. **Tune your sax for every new mouthpiece.**
- **Used mouthpieces** are available too. Always clean them before you try them, and carefully inspect them for dents, chips, and other damage – especially the rails.
- When it comes to mouthpieces, **thousandths of an inch** can make a difference. That's why no two mouthpieces are exactly the same – even if they are 'identical' – so always try out a few before you decide.

Mouthpieces and reeds

- When you are testing mouthpieces, be sure to always use **a good, new reed**.
- A new mouthpiece may ask for **different reeds** than the ones you were using – harder reeds, softer ones, or even reeds of a different brand.
- Note that some mouthpieces are more **reed-friendly** than others. With one mouthpiece, eight out of ten reeds will do well, while another makes you reject five out of ten.
- Also, a mouthpiece won't perform to its full potential until you have found the right reed to go with it. A good salesperson can advise you on **good reed/mouthpiece combinations**.

Brand names

There are dozens of mouthpiece brands. Most saxophone brands have their own mouthpieces, which they don't always make themselves. Many other, smaller companies specialize in mouthpieces, some of the better-known names being JJ Babbitt (Meyer, Guy Hawkins, Otto Link, Wolfe Tayne), Bari, Berg Larsen, Dukoff, Guardala, Hite, Lakey, Lamberson, François Louis, Ponzol, Rousseau, and Runyon. Companies such as Brancher and Vandoren make both mouthpieces and reeds. Some of these companies offer mouthpieces for every style of music, and in various price ranges, while others are mostly known for their loud and bright-sounding mouthpieces, or for ensemble-oriented models, or for expensive or beginners' mouthpieces only. Still others feature special designs such as an adjustable lay, an integrated ligature, or a built-in metal reed that enhances the tone and loudness of your sax.

How many?

Some saxophonists buy a good mouthpiece once and play it for the rest of their lives. Others never stop trying new models, brands, and types. Likewise, there are those who have a vast collection of mouthpieces to adapt their sound to different halls, groups, or styles of music, while others handle a similar variety of situations with just one mouthpiece…

LIGATURES

Even the ligature contributes to your sound. Ligatures mainly differ in the material used, and in how they hold the reed.

One or two

Some ligatures use two screws, others have only one. The difference is not that big. One-screw designs are easier to attach or remove. Two screws are sometimes said to ensure a more even distribution of pressure across the reed – but one-screw designs can be just as good or even better.

Inverted

An *inverted ligature* has screws not in the usual location, at the bottom of the mouthpiece, but on top, opposite the reed. This supposedly allows the reed to move more freely, and therefore to respond more easily.

Material

Besides conventional metal ligatures, there are models in leather, soft plastic, textile, metal mesh, and metal wire. The softer and thicker the material, the more it will tend to make your horn sound darker, warmer, and smoother. If you want to hear what a soft ligature can do for you, try attaching your reed with a shoestring or a piece of duct tape.

Interchangeable plates

The smaller the contact area between ligature and reed, the more freely it can vibrate. This makes for a bright, open sound and a fast response. Some ligatures have inter-changeable plates that hold the reed in various ways – with metal strips, or with four small points only, for example – allowing you to adapt your sound to the music or the venue.

A standard metal ligature and a soft one (BG).

Tips and tricks

Standard ligatures can also be 'adjusted,' to some extent. If
you have a reed that is a bit too light, tighten the upper
screw a bit less. That allows a longer section of the reed to
vibrate, which has an effect similar to that of a slightly
heavier reed. There are more tips and tricks on mounting
reeds in Chapter 9, *Before and after*.

Bite

Two more things to pay attention to: Some types of
ligature allow you to vary the exact position of the reed
very easily, even without (re)moving the ligature itself.
Others don't. Another difference is that some ligatures
'bite' into the reed. Once a reed has been fixed, it won't be
easy to change its position again.

A neat fit

Whichever ligature you choose, make sure it fits your
mouthpiece. With a poorly fitting ligature the reed may
slip out of place, or not seal to the mouthpiece correctly.
A tip: A different ligature usually requires a different
mouthpiece cap.

Prices and brands

The cheapest standard ligatures are available for five to ten
dollars. Expect to pay ten to twenty if you want something
better, and twice to four times that amount if you want
something special. Almost all saxophone and mouthpiece
makers and some reed makers have their own ligatures, and
there are also specialized accessory makers such as BG,
Harrison, Oleg, Rovner, Runyon, Tru-Blo, and Winslow.

8. REEDS

What strings are to guitarists and violinists, reeds are to saxophonists. They are important for the way you sound and play, you need to replace them frequently, and there are all kinds of tricks to make them last as long as possible.

The main difference between one reed and the other is how soft or hard they are. Most manufacturers classify their reeds with numbers, usually from 1 to 5, in half steps. The higher the number, the harder or more resistant the reed.

Harder
Harder reeds allow for a louder, heavier, darker, thicker, or fuller sound, but they require good breath control and a developed embouchure. A hard reed makes it harder to play low pitches softly.

Softer
With a softer reed, playing softly is easier. A soft reed speaks more easily and gives a bright, lighter sound. If it's too soft, the sound may get very thin or buzzy. With soft reeds, there's a greater chance that the pitch will go up and down as you play, so it's harder to play in tune.

Same thickness
Contrary to common belief, a reed #2 is not thinner than a 4 of the same brand and series. It's simply made of a softer, less resistant piece of cane. Softer reeds have a shorter play life. Eventually, most saxophonists go for a 3, a 3½, or an even harder reed.

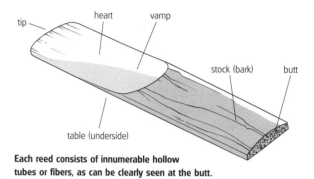

Each reed consists of innumerable hollow
tubes or fibers, as can be clearly seen at the butt.

Number two?

Good to know: A reed #2 from one brand or series may be
equivalent to a 1½ or a 2½ from another brand or series.
As with mouthpieces, there are tables that list various types
of reeds side by side. Some brands use names (*e.g.*, soft,
medium, hard, etc.) instead of numbers.

Your mouthpiece

Which reed to choose depends on various factors, your
mouthpiece being one of them. For example, a smaller tip
opening requires a heavier reed. With a reed that's too soft,
it will close up and not respond at all. Conversely, a
mouthpiece with a large tip opening will play easier with
a lighter reed. For beginners the best choice often is a
medium-soft reed, such as a 2 or a 2½, on a mouthpiece
with a medium-small tip opening.

Good and bad

Almost every box of reeds contains great reeds and good
reeds, average and poor ones. If the boxes you buy seem
consistently short of good reeds, try a different brand or a
different type – and be sure that the problem doesn't
lie somewhere else. If your mouthpiece is crooked or
damaged, or if your instrument is leaking, any reed will
seem poor.

Not equally hard

Of course ten 'identical' reeds from one and the same box
won't all be equally hard. A box of reeds #2½ will contain
reeds that are just a little harder than a 'hard' 2, as well as
some that come close to a 'soft' 3.

Thicker, steeper
How a reed plays and sounds also depends on its design: the thickness of the heart, the way it slopes toward the edges, and so on.

French and American cuts
For example, reeds can be divided into *French cut* and *American cut* reeds. French cut reeds, which are mainly used by classical saxophonists, have a thinner tip and they're a bit thicker in the heart area. Reeds with an American cut usually feature a slightly thicker tip and less heart, which produces a more massive, focused sound.

American?
However, these terms are not as neatly defined as they may seem. Just take a close look at a number of 'American cut' reeds from a variety of brands, and you'll find at least as many differences as similarities.

French file cut
Reeds with a *file cut* or *double cut* have an extra strip of the bark removed, in a straight line, right behind the vamp. This enhances the flexibility of the reed, making for an easier response, especially in the low register. Also it helps produce a brighter, more narrowly focused sound. As this technique was developed in France, where

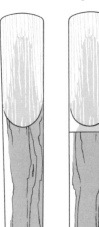

classical musicians have always appreciated a brighter sound, it's known as *French file cut* – which shouldn't be mixed up with the French cut reeds mentioned above. The 'regular' or *unfiled* cut is sometimes referred to as *single cut*.

Fine-tuning
The choice between filed and unfiled reeds can help you fine-tune your sound, regardless of the style you're playing. Saxophonists with a darker-sounding mouthpiece may want to use filed reeds, while unfiled

Reeds with and without a (French) file cut.

reeds are often used on mouthpieces that tend to produce a brighter sound.

Many more
Of course there are many more bigger and smaller differences. Some types of reeds have been developed for a well-rounded, centered, classical sound, while others are meant to blow easily with lots of color, expressiveness, and volume. Likewise, some reeds can handle fast phrases and powerful licks better than others that are better suited for performing long, steady notes – and so on. Most companies offer helpful descriptions of what their various designs were meant for. However, don't be surprised if you meet musicians who successfully use reeds that were designed for a completely different style of playing than theirs.

Which type of reed?
Each brand makes different types of reeds. The only way to find out which reed you like best is to try a lot of them. Trading experiences with other saxophonists can help too, but remember that no two players are alike. Also, a reed that works brilliantly with one mouthpiece can be hopeless on another. Another tip: Always try a couple of reeds of each type. One poor reed tells you nothing.

Prices
Most saxophonists who have found 'their' reed buy them in boxes of five or ten. Soprano, alto and tenor reeds typically cost between two and four dollars each, and you may be able to get them for a dollar. Baritone reeds often start around four dollars.

EXAMINING REEDS
You'll find good, average, and poor reeds in almost every box. Careful examination can often weed out the bad ones pretty easily.

Inverted V
If you hold up a reed to the light, you'll see an inverted V. That V must be centered, and the reed should get thinner evenly to both sides. 'Crooked' reeds may squeak, and they're hard to play.

| Good V-shape: can sound good. | A 'crooked' reed, risk of squeaks. | Uneven grain: better not to buy it. | Knots: reed vibrates unevenly. |

Flexibility
By carefully sliding your thumb and index finger along the sides of the reed, you can tell whether the flexibility of the reed is the same on both sides.

Too young
The color of a good reed varies between gold-yellow and gold-brown. If there's a hint of green, the reed may be too young. Young reeds usually won't last long or play well, if at all. Do not reject them right away, but let them sit for a few months at least.

Grain and knots
The grain should be even throughout the reed, with the fibers densely packed, running evenly and parallel to one another. Reeds with spots and knots are unlikely to vibrate evenly.

Wet it first
You won't know how good a reed is until you have been playing it for a while. A dry reed doesn't vibrate properly, so always wet it first. Keep it in your mouth for a while or put it in a glass of clean, lukewarm water for a few minutes. The latter method may extend the life of a reed: Some say water is better for reeds than saliva – but others disagree.

Glass
You can also lay the reed on a wet piece of glass or mirror. Some reed cases have a special bottom for this purpose.

The glass helps to keep the reed flat, removing waves or wrinkles at the tip. Don't use Plexiglas, as it's difficult to keep clean.

Breaking them in

Reeds that perform very well straight away may not last very long. The best reeds are often the ones that seem a little hard to begin with. In other words, they don't play well right away. That's why some saxophonists first 'break in' their new reeds, for instance by only using them a few minutes per day for the first week. They may also use that breaking-in period to adjust the reed if necessary – a little bit every day. Some experts advise that you massage new reeds, sliding your thumb over the vamp, down to the tip, which may be helpful if a reed feels too stiff. Others don't bother with such procedures at all: If a reed doesn't play well, they simply take another one.

Double plus, double minus

When you're testing a box of new reeds, give each reed a grade, or give the best reeds two plusses, the worst ones two minuses, and so on. Don't throw away the 'bad' reeds, but let them sit for a few months: Sometimes they will improve with age, and they never get too old. You can also try adjusting the poorer ones, or experiment a little with the placement of the reed on the mouthpiece (see page 83).

Swapping reeds

Reeds are said to last longer if you don't use the same one for too long at a stretch. For that purpose, some sax players carry a supply of good reeds, which allows them to switch reeds every hour or even more frequently. Swapping reeds has yet another advantage: If you use one reed all the time, it will gradually become weaker. By the time the reed 'goes,' it will be so weak that any new reed you try will seem too hard.

Suddenly

If you rotate your reeds regularly, you will also get a better feel for the slight differences between 'identical' reeds. What's more, you'll always have plenty of good reeds on hand – which is useful, because even the best reed can give up suddenly.

Different reeds

You can also use these slight differences (or even use different strengths or types of reeds) to adapt to various playing conditions – for example, a harder-playing reed when humidity is very high, or in resonant or large venues. A lighter-playing reed works better in dry air, dry acoustics, and small rooms. In other words: The reed that sounds great in a small, insulated practice studio may not be the best reed for your next concert.

ADJUSTING REEDS

Some saxophonists adjust every reed themselves; others do so only if it is really necessary, or not at all. Learning to adjust reeds takes a lot of time and patience, and you'll use up a lot of – bad or average – reeds doing it. A few important tips are listed below; some of the books on pages 125–126 discuss this subject at greater length.

Higher, lower, or crooked

Before adjusting a reed, try to solve the problem by varying its exact position on the mouthpiece. A reed that doesn't seem to work well when it is put on perfectly straight may suddenly start sounding good if you mount it a little higher, a little lower, or at a slight angle – in which case adjustment will no longer be necessary. Want to know more? See page 83.

Flat
Tipcode SAX-013

If you have a reed whose *facing* (the part in contact with the mouthpiece) is not perfectly flat or even, you can sand it down. Lay a piece of very fine grade sandpaper (number 320 or finer) on a small plate of glass to make sure it is level, or get a whetstone (*carborundum stone*) instead. Move the reed over it lengthways along the grain of the reed, with smooth and even motions, or carefully sand it in a circular motion, both clockwise and counterclockwise. Exert as little pressure as possible and don't let the tip touch the stone. Some people scour the reed with a sharp penknife instead, pulling the blade across the reed a few times.

Too soft
Tipcode SAX-014

A reed that's too soft can leave you with a messy, unsteady tone, or make a tone stop abruptly. The solution is to cut down the tip of the reed with a *reed cutter* or *reed trimmer*. Cut off as little as possible at first, and don't cut it down more than 0.04" to 0.06" (1–1.5 mm). Remember to first wet the reed. Afterwards, you may need to smooth the corners a little. To do so, use a file, always moving it towards the center of the reed. Most reed cutters cost around twenty to fifty dollars.

Too hard
Tipcode SAX-015

If a reed is too hard, you can make it more flexible by scraping it with a sharp knife or a piece of *reed rush* or *Dutch rush*, sold in music stores. Start in the areas marked with the figure 1 – carefully, because the reed is already very thin at this point. If necessary, go on to the areas marked 2, then to 3 and 4. Always remove equal amounts left and right, otherwise you will push the reed out of balance.

Shrill or dull

You can try rescuing a shrill-sounding reed by adjusting the areas marked 3 and 4. On dull-sounding reeds you start at 1, then move on to 3 and 4, and possibly try 2 as well.

Squeak

Squeaking reeds are often not equally flexible or thick on the left and the right. In the latter case you can try making the thicker edge a little thinner. Keep checking how much you have removed by blowing with the mouthpiece at an angle in your mouth: First try it left, then right.

Tips

• Work carefully: It's easy to remove **too much material**. For example, taking as little as a few ten thousandths of an inch off the tip of a reed makes it a whole 10% thinner!

• Frequently **check your results** as you work. Instead of constantly taking the ligature off and putting it back on again, you can temporarily hold the reed in place with your thumb.

• Some reeds will **never be any good**, however much you work on them.

- As a rule, avoid the area marked X, the **heart of the reed**.
- If you want to tackle the job really seriously, you can buy special reed **adjustment devices and kits** with prices up to three hundred dollars.
- And finally: **Waves at the tip** of the reed will disappear when you play it for a while, or if you briefly put the reed in a glass of water.

Pith and saliva

A reed consists of countless hollow miniature tubes or fibers with a soft material (*pith*) between them. The pith becomes gradually softer from exposure to your saliva, until it gets so soft that the reed stops working altogether. How long that takes depends on the type of saliva you have, how often you play, and on the reed itself. Reeds typically last between two and six weeks.

Increasing the lifetime

There are all kinds of ways you can try to increase the life expectancy of your reeds.

- Rinse your reed **in clean water** after playing. Then dry it, for instance with a cotton cloth or handkerchief, or by passing it between your thumb and index finger, always towards the tip. However, most saxophonists just dry the reed, without rinsing it first.
- Always store your reeds in a good **reed case or reed guard** (see page 88).
- Lay each new reed on a flat surface and firmly rub it from the heart to the tip with the back of a teaspoon. This **closes the fibers** in the reed, which enhances its life expectancy.
- Don't play **the same reed** too long.
- **Break your reeds in**, so that the dried material gradually gets used to being wet again.
- **Hydrogen peroxide** solution (3%, available from your local drugstore) counteracts the effect of your saliva on the reed. Put your reeds in the solution overnight once in a while, and rinse them well before you use them again.
- **Never** set down a mouthpiece with a reed in it vertically. Lay it on its side, so that it can't fall over. That'll save on broken reeds.
- **Taking a break**? A mouthpiece cap protects your reed and keeps it moist.

REED BRANDS

Rico (US) also makes reeds under the LaVoz and Mitchell Lurie names. The companies Brancher, Glotin, Marca, Rigotti, Selmer (also makes saxes), and Vandoren (also makes mouthpieces) are from France, which is where most of the reed cane grows. Some other brand names are Alexander Superial, Daniel's, Olivieri, Peter Ponzol (makes mouthpieces too), Reeds Australia, RKM, and Zonda.

Synthetic reeds

Synthetic or plastic reeds are also available – for example, from the brands Bari, Fibracell, Hartmann (Fiberreed), Légère, Olivieri, and RKM. They last much longer and they're much more consistent than cane reeds. Another advantage is that you don't have to wet them before playing, which is especially easy if you have to switch instruments within one song. Synthetic reeds produce a loud, bright, and powerful sound. They're usually not an ideal choice for beginners, as they're quite resistant and hard to control, and they can present intonation problems.

Expensive

Synthetic reeds are a good deal more expensive than cane, with prices between five and twenty dollars each. Also, many players feel that they tend to sound shrill, harsh, or edgy, but remember that it's a fairly new product and that is being improved upon all the time.

Coatings and mixes

Some other reed variations are cane reeds with a plastic coating, or reeds that are made of a mix of natural fibers and synthetics. Like synthetic reeds, they're usually designed to outlast cane reeds and offer a brighter, more powerful sound.

Tasty

Don't you like the taste of cane? Then try some of the flavored reeds available, or buy a bottle of reed flavoring. Both products are available in various flavors.

9. BEFORE AND AFTER

A chapter about all the things you need to do to your saxophone before and after playing, from putting it together to tuning it, taking it apart, and storing it, with tips on amplification, stands, and lyres. Polishing, cleaning, adjusting, and other less frequent types of maintenance are dealt with in Chapter 10.

To assemble your horn, start by attaching the reed to the mouthpiece, then put the mouthpiece on the neck and the neck on the body – but you can do it any other way around as well. This chapter starts with putting on the reed.

In four steps   Tipcode SAX-016

1. Slide the ligature onto the mouthpiece, holding it a bit higher than where it will eventually be positioned.
2. Slide the wetted reed (see page 76) under the ligature.
3. Make sure that the reed lines up with the mouthpiece, both at the tip and the sides. Then slide the ligature into position.
4. Tighten the ligature screw(s) – not too much, otherwise the reed won't vibrate properly.

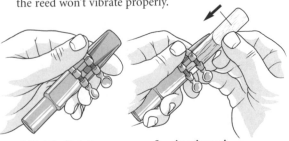

1 First the ligature...   2 ... then the reed.

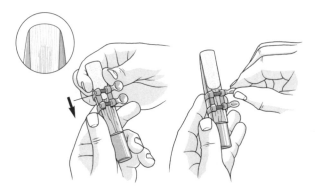

3 Check the reed's position...   4 ... then tighten the ligature.

The ligature

Both the mouthpiece and the ligature are a bit wider on one end than on the other, so always make sure you put the ligature on the right way around. Many mouthpieces have a guideline that shows you how far the ligature should be pushed down. Using another type of ligature may render this line irrelevant, of course.

Too light, too heavy?

You may vary the position of the ligature to compensate for a reed that plays too lightly or too heavily. A reed will behave as if it were a little harder if you slide down the ligature a bit, or loosen the screw closest to the reed a little.

Positioning the reed

You can also try moving the reed itself up (if it feels too soft) or down the mouthpiece (if it feels too hard) a little. Reeds that are not perfectly even left and right will often perform better if you set them on your mouthpiece at a slight angle.

Body and neck

The safest way to remove your sax from its case is to grasp it by the bell with one hand, supporting it with the other. Don't grab it by the key system, to prevent bending things. Put the neck into the body with a gentle twisting motion. If the neck doesn't slide into the body smoothly, clean the receiver (the top part of the body) and the neck tenon with a dry cloth only. The small screw of the receiver should, like the ligature screws, not be fastened too tightly.

Swivel

Many saxophonists don't hold their horn directly in front of them, but off to the right a bit. To do so, swivel the neck slightly to the left. Make sure the octave mechanism is still lined up.

Cork grease

If the mouthpiece doesn't slide over the neck smoothly, the neck cork needs a little *cork grease*. Always have some with you (see page 99).

Warming up

A cold sax doesn't respond very well, and it will sound a little flat (too low). You can warm it up by blowing a few long, slow, silent breaths through the instrument, keeping all keys closed. If your sax has become very cold in transit, speed up the process by inserting a small towel into the bell.

Brushing and flossing, food and drinks

If you want to spend as little time as possible on maintaining your instrument, then wash your hands and brush and floss your teeth before you play, don't eat during intermissions, and don't drink anything that contains sugar. It helps, really.

The neckstrap

Adjust the neckstrap so that the mouthpiece swings directly to your mouth, without you having to stoop down or strain upward to reach it. If there's too much weight on your thumb, or if you have to face down, your neckstrap is too long – which may also hinder your sound. If you find yourself tilting your head backward, make the strap a bit longer. Invest some time to find the right neckstrap length: It may save you from chronic neck problems and other symptoms.

Sticky pads?

Pads can stick, especially the ones that are closed when at rest. Short- and long-term remedies are covered on page 98.

TUNING

A saxophone needs to be tuned, even if you play by yourself. If you don't tune it, the instrument's intonation will be off.

Adjusting the mouthpiece

You tune a sax by simply pushing the mouthpiece further onto the neck. This makes the entire instrument a bit shorter, and thus a bit higher in pitch. Moving the mouthpiece back makes the instrument longer, lowering the pitch. It's easy to remember: the longer the horn, the lower the pitch.

Extreme tunings

If your horn is tuned way too high or too low, you may have intonation problems, as the position of the toneholes won't match the total length of the horn anymore. If the mouthpiece is too far back, your low register will sound sloppy as well.

Concert A

Most orchestras and bands tune to the note A4. This is the A above Middle C on a piano.

A=440   Tipcode SAX-017

At this pitch the air vibrates 440 times per second, indicated as 440 hertz.

Tuning fork or metronome   Tipcode SAX-018

Rather than using a piano, you can produce this reference pitch with a tuning fork. Tap it against your knee and set its stem on a tabletop, or hold it against or near your ear. Tuning forks are available in different tunings, so make sure you get one tuned to A=440. A tip: Most electronic metronomes and tuning devices can play this pitch too.

Alto and tenor sax

- To sound this A on an alto, you should finger an F♯, with the octave key depressed.
- On a tenor you finger a B, also using the octave key.

An A on a keyboard.

An A concert pitch on an alto (fingered F♯).

An A concert pitch on a tenor (fingered B).

Tune to B♭

Some saxophonists prefer to tune to other pitches. One example is to tune an alto to a concert B♭, using a B♭ tuning fork. Why? Because you can finger the required G with one hand only, so you can play the tuning fork with the other. To tune a tenor or a soprano to this tuning fork, you have to finger a C.

Far in, far out   Tipcode SAX-019

If you're a beginner, it may be difficult to hear whether your instrument sounds flat or sharp. Here's a trick: First push the mouthpiece as far onto the neck as it will go. Now the instrument will sound obviously sharp. Then pull it out as far as possible, making it sound flat. The correct tuning will be somewhere in the middle.

Electronic tuners

Most electronic tuners have a built-in microphone that 'hears' what you play and registers it on the dial as sharp, flat, or just right. Apart from tuning purposes, electronic tuners are also used to check an instrument's intonation or to practice voicing notes. Many experts disapprove of the latter, by the way: Electronic tuners (and keyboard instruments, for example) don't differentiate between an F♯ and a G♭. Wind players should though, for reasons that go beyond the scope of this book.

Special tuners

There are special tuners for transposing instruments. Shift it to the pitch your instrument is in and it will display the note you're fingering, rather than the sounding note. Another tip: Some tuners automatically switch off after a couple of minutes, which saves on batteries. And one more: There are tuners that clip onto your instrument and respond to the vibrations of the horn instead of using a microphone. These allow you to tune in noisy surroundings.

Higher temperature, higher pitch

A sax will warm up with playing, so you may have to retune after a while: A higher temperature results in a higher pitch. If it's steaming hot or freezing cold, it may be hard to get the instrument to play in tune at all.

Tuning line

Is your sax warmed up and well tuned? Draw a line on the neck cork or *tuning cork*, just where the mouthpiece ends. The next time you play, simply align the mouthpiece to the line. Then your tuning can't be that far off.

Paper, thread, or match

If the tuning cork has gotten so compressed that your mouthpiece doesn't fit properly any more, simply wrap some thin paper around it. Cigarette paper is perfect. As an alternative you can wrap some thread around the cork, and then rub it with a candle. Others warm the cork with a lighter, for example. (Be careful, as cork burns easily.) The best solution is to have the neck recorked.

AFTERWARDS

Taking proper care of your instrument when you're done playing will make it last longer – especially the pads – and it'll save spending time and money on more serious types of maintenance.

Reed

Reeds last longest if you rinse and dry them after playing (see page 80). If you leave your reed on the mouthpiece, it won't dry as easily, which will make it more likely to warp. Besides, you'll have to take it off to wet it next time you play anyway.

Reed cases

You can store the reed in a very basic open reed holder or in a reed guard with some type of lid, both available for a couple of dollars, or get yourself a deluxe, leather-clad reed case for fifty dollars, or something in between. If you're used to changing your reeds frequently, or if you use different reeds for different situations, get a reed case with numbered compartments. This will help you to tell your reeds apart.

Wet, dry...

Reeds will dry most evenly in a reed case with ventilation holes and a ribbed floor, so that the air can get everywhere. Other cases have glass floors that help to prevent waves from forming at the tip of the reed. What works best may depend on the reeds you use, and on how wet or dry they are when you store them. Some holders have replaceable cartridges containing a substance that keeps the humidity at the right level.

Moisture control

If humidity is very low, you can store your reeds in special moisture-controlled cases, some even featuring built-in hygrometers. A less expensive alternative is to keep your reed guard in a freezer box or zip freezer bag, which will help to prevent the reeds from drying out. Tip: Reeds can go moldy if you keep them in a case that's completely closed.

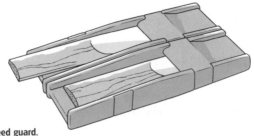

A reed guard.

Moisture

When you play, the moisture in your breath condenses, wetting the inside of the instrument and the pads. To remove the moisture, you can use a swab, a pad saver, or both.

Pad saver

A *pad saver* is a long fluffy plume that you move in and out of your sax a couple of times. Some saxophonists dislike pad savers because they tend to leave behind fibers that can stick on the pads or in the mechanism, because they may spread the moisture around rather than absorbing it, or because their rod can damage the inside of the body.

pad saver

Note, however, that pad savers come in different qualities. Prices start at about ten dollars. As an alternative, some use a wooden rod with a cloth attached to it.

Pull-through swab

A pull-through swab consists of a cloth attached to a cord with a small weight on the other end. The cloth may be chamois, silk, or cotton. Simply drop the weight down the instrument and pull the swab through it a couple of times. The metal weight should be wrapped to prevent damage.

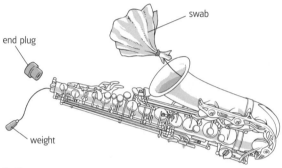

swab

end plug

weight

Both

There are players who combine a swab and a pad saver, leaving the latter in the instrument once it has been dried with the first. Others, however, dislike the idea of leaving the pad saver in the horn, believing that it will collect dust and may dry out the pads too much.

At home

Whether you use a pad saver or a swab, it's good to leave the case open just a bit once you come home. This allows the pads to dry slowly – unless air humidity is very low.

The outside

To prevent stains and tarnish, it's advisable to wipe the instrument down with a soft, dry cloth after playing. Don't forget the neck and the little finger keys.

End plug

The *end plug* protects the octave key rod – the small post that protrudes from the top of the body. End plugs can be made of rubber, plastic, metal, wood, or cork. Simply insert it into the body before packing up.

The neck and mouthpiece

An ordinary handkerchief is all you need to dry the mouthpiece. It's even better if you rinse the mouthpiece in lukewarm water before you do. There are special swabs available too, both for the mouthpiece and the neck.

CASES AND BAGS

Saxophone cases can be shaped (contoured or form-fitting cases) or rectangular, with a hard or a soft shell. Various materials are used to absorb shocks. A plush or velvet lining prevents scratching the instrument.

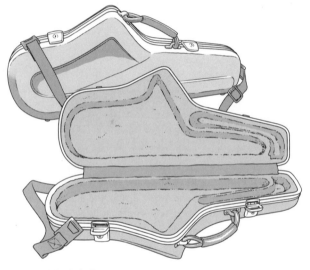

A shaped hard-shell case.

More space

Good hard-shell cases usually have a strong plywood or molded plastic core. Rectangular models offer more space than shaped cases, with separate compartments for your neck, mouthpiece, strap, extra reeds, and accessories, and sometimes for sheet music as well. In a shaped case, usually featuring a hard plastic shell, the mouthpiece and neck often need to be stored in the bell (see below).

Gig bag

A *gig bag* is a thickly lined bag, often made of water-resistant synthetic cloth, and subtly shaped for the instrument.

Gig bags often have one or more extra pockets, as well as shoulder or backpack straps. Most gig bags won't protect your instrument as well as a good hard-shell case does, but gig bags are more comfortable to carry around.

Tight fit
To prevent damage, your horn should fit its case tightly, so that it can't shift around. On the other hand, if the case is too small, it can push too tightly against the instrument and bend its keys or rods. For the same reason, never store sheet music on top of your horn.

Locked
Most cases can be locked. More than anything, these small locks are there to prevent the lid from springing open if the case falls. A separate case cover (Cordura, canvas, leather) will do that too, as well as offering additional protection against rain and dirt.

Locks and hinges
Check to see how sturdy latches, locks, zips, hinges, and handles are: They tend to be the weak points on cases and gig bags. Plastic clips and rings may not be as strong as metal ones.

Neck and mouthpiece
If you store the neck and mouthpiece in the instrument's bell, you need to package them separately – and it's a good idea to do so if you store them elsewhere in your case too. There are special, inexpensive, high quality pouches with separate pockets for mouthpieces and necks, but many sax players simply wrap them up in lint-free cloths or gym socks.

Preventing tarnish
To prevent silver-plated horns from tarnishing quickly, you can put special silver protectant paper strips in your case or bag.

Prices
The cheapest gig bags are available for some fifty dollars or even less, moving up to three hundred for a genuine leather one. Decent alto or tenor cases, either rectangular or shaped,

usually start around a hundred dollars, going up to three or four hundred dollars. Higher-priced cases are usually much more protective and can save on lots of money in repairs.

Key clamps

If you really want to be safe, use *key clamps* or *sax clamps* when you store your instrument: These sets of clips and pliers keep the open-standing keys closed for transportation, offering additional protection against bent keys and rods. They install and de-install in seconds.

Always

Always store your sax in its case or bag – even at home. Apart from offering protection, this will also prevent airborne dust from clogging the key system. Whether or not the instrument is in its case or bag, always make sure it doesn't get too hot, so keep it out of direct sunlight and away from other sources of heat.

MISCELLANEOUS

A few odds and ends at the end of this chapter: neckstraps, saxophone stands, lyres, microphones, and some tips for on the road.

Neckstraps

The traditional, narrow type of neckstrap isn't very comfortable. Many modern designs are considerably wider, and they often feature – sometimes removable – padding that evenly distributes the instrument's weight over your neck and shoulders. Other straps are designed to sit lower on your shoulders, rather than around your neck. Straps with a stretch backing are also available. Some musicians like the flexible feel; others don't.

Harness and braces

If you want to avoid putting a strain on your neck entirely, buy a *harness*, which fits over your shoulders and around your waist. They may not be easy to get into or make you look great, but they're extremely comfortable and may save you a lot of pain. Harnesses or *dual shoulder straps* are particularly advisable for younger players. One more alternative are braces that attach to your clothes like a pair of suspenders. Prices range from less than ten dollars for a basic neckstrap to some fifty dollars for a harness.

A regular neckstrap, a brace, and a harness.

Hooks
Pay some attention to the hook too. Many saxophonists go for the most straightforward type, basically a bent piece of hardened steel wire with a plastic coating to keep it from scratching your instrument.

Spring hooks
Other hooks employ some kind of spring action. They're usually considered to be more reliable, but they take more time when changing instruments. Some of these hooks can swivel around freely, so the strap doesn't get twisted.

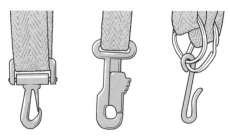

A spring hook, a snap hook, and a regular hook.

One hand
Watch out for the cheapest plastic hooks (they may break), and for hooks that may open inadvertently or allow the sax to work itself loose. An important tip: Always support your sax with one hand when you're not playing, and don't rely entirely on the strap. Another one: Never carry your sax around holding it by the neck – it may come off.

Saxophone support

There's an alternative for the neckstrap when you play sitting down: a saxophone support, consisting of a wide, curved Plexiglas strip that sits *under* your left upper leg and over your right *upper* leg. An adjustable hook mounted on the right-hand side of the strip supports the instrument.

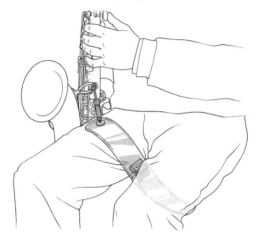

The Saxophone Support.

Stands

Intermission? Use a mouthpiece cap to protect your reed and keep it wet, and put your sax in a safe place – on a sax stand, for example. Good stands have soft bumpers and pretty long legs for stability; they are sturdy, easily collapsible, and easy to transport. Some can be raised to standing height, but this makes them a lot bigger, of course. Prices range from about twenty-five to fifty dollars. Combination stands (*e.g.*, alto, tenor, and clarinet or flute) are available for doublers. Safety tip: On crowded stages it's advisable to attach the stand to the floor using duct tape.

Sax stand.

Lyre

Marching sax players can attach a music stand to their instruments. These *lyres* come in many different versions, some very basic, others with well-designed wind and rain resistant features.

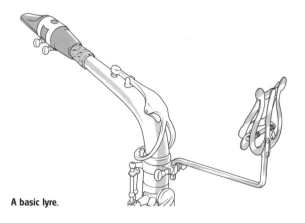

A basic lyre.

AMPLIFICATION

If you play in an 'electric' band, your instrument needs to be amplified. For the occasional event you can use a good vocal microphone. If you need amplification more often, you may consider a special saxophone miking system.

Saxophone mics

Most of these systems use a small clip-on microphone that attaches to the rim or the back of the bell, often with a

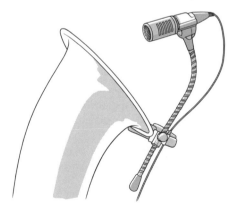

Sax microphone, mounted on the bell of the instrument (SD Systems).

flexible gooseneck to adjust its position. Others have two microphones. Prices vary from around two to five hundred dollars. Cordless systems allow even more freedom to move around but cost a lot more.

Preamplifier

Because the type of microphone used often produces a very weak signal, it usually needs a separate preamplifier – a small box that attaches to your clothing. The preamp, which usually features volume and tone controls, sends the signal to the power amplifier.

(Dis)advantages

These dedicated systems give you more freedom to move around than a microphone on a stand, without changing sound or volume. On the other hand, if your microphone is on a stand, you can deliberately influence volume and tone by changing the distance between the mic and your instrument.

ON THE ROAD

Some additional safety tips:

- Don't put a saxophone on the **luggage shelf of a car**, under the rear window – especially not on a hot day.
- Getting out of the car? Always **take your instrument with you**.
- All kinds of things – including saxes – get left behind on the **luggage racks** of buses, trains, and subways. Tip: Keep hold of your instrument.
- Consider **insuring your instrument**, especially if you take it on the road – which includes visiting your teacher. Musical instruments fall under the insurance category of 'valuables.' A regular homeowner insurance policy will usually not cover all possible damage, whether it occurs at home, on the road, in the studio, or onstage.
- To get your instrument insured you'll need to know the **serial number** and some other details. You can list them on pages 128–129. Insurance companies also often ask for an appraisal report (see page 29) and proof of purchase.

10. CLEANING AND MAINTENANCE

If you conscientiously follow the tips in the preceding chapter, your saxophone will require little further maintenance. A bit of extra cleaning now and again, and perhaps the odd drop of oil – that's all there is to it. Once in a while, though, you will need to take it to a technician for a COA (cleaning, oiling, and adjusting) or an overhaul. Here's what you can do yourself and what you should leave to a professional.

To get rid of fingerprints and dust, wipe down the instrument with a dry or slightly damp, soft, lint-free cloth. Use a small soft brush for the tricky places, and be careful not to hurt your fingers: The needle springs are very sharp. This process is not cosmetic only: Dust may build up in the hinges and eventually clog up the key system, slowing down the action and causing excessive wear. To prevent dust from settling in the mechanism it's also advisable to vacuum your case once in a while.

No polish

Don't use metal polishes on lacquered instruments. It wears down the lacquer coating in no time, and it can get into the hinges, gumming up the key system, and on the pads. On silver-plated saxes you may, very carefully, use a silver-polishing cloth once in a while: The extremely thin silver plating wears down easily.

Your mouthpiece

Lukewarm water is often enough to clean your mouthpiece, and you may want to use a special mouthpiece brush, with some liquid hand soap or a mild dishwashing detergent. Adding a small amount of domestic cleaning vinegar works against the buildup of scale – and scale may very well hold disagreeable residues. Never leave a hard rubber mouthpiece in hot water or a vinegar solution. It won't fall apart, but chances are it will discolor.

Swab and pad saver
A swab or pad saver gets a lot of junk out of your horn, so wash it from time to time with warm water and a mild detergent, and let it dry thoroughly.

Sticking pads   Tipcode SAX-020
Pads can stick – especially the ones that are closed when at rest. Fix them by sticking a piece of regular paper, a handkerchief, or a lens cleaning cloth under the pad, and then gently push the key cup down a few times. If that doesn't do the trick, try carefully pulling the paper out from under the pad while you keep it lightly closed with your finger on the key cup.

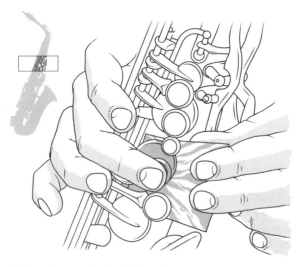

Stick it under the pad, close lightly, pull out...

Dollar bills, tissues, talcum powder
Instead of plain paper, a dollar bill may work even better, as it is a bit rough. Cigarette paper or good quality paper tissues can be used too. Some saxophonists apply a bit of

talcum powder to the pad with a Q-tip (cotton bud) or an old reed. However, the powder may render the pad even stickier when it gets moist. Also, it can find its way into the mechanism, where it can mix with the oil to form a sticky mass.

Softening pads
Leather pads get harder with age. Various liquids, usually marketed as *pad dope* or *pad juice*, are available to help reduce this effect.

Cork grease
Applying a bit of *cork grease* on the neck cork prevents it from drying out, eases putting the mouthpiece on the neck, and provides a good seal. Cork grease comes in small containers and lipstick-type tubes. Some use Vaseline or light machine oils instead, but you can't go much cheaper than cork grease, which has the added benefit of being designed for the purpose.

Oiling the keywork
Music stores sell special cleaning sets for saxes. Besides a swab, a cloth, and one or two brushes, they often include a bottle of key oil. Some manufacturers advise you to put a *tiny* drop of oil on the hinges once a month or every two months.

Don't do it yourself
Many technicians prefer you not to do that yourself, for one thing because oiling only really helps if you first take the mechanism apart and clean it. There's also the risk that you'll use too much oil or get oil on the pads, or use oil that is too thick or too runny for your instrument. So if you want to be on the safe side, leave it to an expert. Once a year or every six months is usually enough, if it's done properly.

Doing it yourself
If you decide to do it yourself anyway, apply the oil with a pin: Drip a drop of oil onto a cigarette paper and dip your pin in it. That way you'll never use too much. As an alternative, there are special oil bottles with a hollow pin on the nozzle.

On the road

There are a few tips that may help you when you're having troubles on the road, and there's no technician around.

- If a key suddenly **stops working**, look at the corresponding spring. If it's broken or gone, a rubber band may temporarily replace it. Always remove the rubber band after playing, as it may damage your plating or lacquer in the long run.
- Has the spring come loose, then reinsert it. A **crochet needle** works well for this purpose.
- **Lost your low register**? Chances are that your neck octave vent is not closing its tonehole. Curing this often requires carefully bending the octave mechanism – which you may prefer to leave to your technician.
- Too much noise? Check for **missing bumpers**. You can reglue them with a drop of water-soluble glue. Other types of glue may harden your felts, spoil your finish, or be so permanent that felts and corks can't be replaced anymore.
- **Squeaks**? Wet the reed, replace the reed, or practice even more...
- **More useful things to take along** when you go out: a spare ligature and mouthpiece (rubber mouthpieces can break; metal ones can dent), cigarette paper, cork grease, a crochet needle, and a few rubber bands. For the technically inclined player there are special toolboxes available, filled with various spare parts and tools.

CHECK-UP

If you get your instrument checked once a year, you can be fairly sure that nothing major can go wrong. Some technicians consider once every two years to be sufficient, depending on how much you play. Expect to pay some fifty to seventy-five dollars for an annual checkup or COA (cleaning, oiling, adjusting). The longer you wait, the more expensive it can get. A tip: Many repair shops will give you a price and time estimate on the repair before checking your instrument into the shop.

Sneaky leaks

Most leaks develop gradually, and you don't notice them coming because you unconsciously adjust your technique to them, squeezing the keys a bit more, blowing a bit harder… Small leaks can often be cured by adjusting one or more keys, or by replacing one or more pads. A few tricks on how to locate leaks are on page 55.

Overhaul

Saxophones need to be overhauled once every five to ten years, mostly, again, depending on how much you play. A complete overhaul usually includes disassembling, cleaning and degreasing the mechanism; cleaning the body and neck inside and out; removing small dents; leveling the toneholes if necessary; replacing pads, bumpers and springs; and reassembling and adjusting the instrument. Expect to pay between three and six hundred dollars. If you decide to have your instrument relacquered or replated, the overhaul is included, of course.

A loan instrument

An overhaul usually means you'll be without your horn for at least a couple of days, and often even longer. Some music stores and repair facilities may provide you with a loan instrument while yours is in the shop. It pays to check this in advance.

Try it out

Whether you take your instrument for a COA or a full overhaul, it will be adjusted. A tip: Try your instrument out before you take it home again, so that you know that it plays the way you want it to. Note that you may have to get used to the instrument feeling different, especially if the adjustment was way off.

11. BACK IN TIME

The saxophone is one of the very few instruments that
were actually invented, rather than developed over time,
and it's only logical that it was named after its inventor.
Adolphe Sax is best known for his saxophone, but he
also invented and developed a host of other instruments
and even some medical equipment.

Of the many stories about what Sax was really
after when working on the saxophone, only one
is correct: He wanted to create an instrument
with the power of a brasswind instrument,
the virtuoso possibilities and the
flexibility of a string instrument, and the
timbre and tonal flexibility of a woodwind
instrument. One of his main inspirations was
the *ophicleide*, a now obsolete brasswind
instrument with a woodwind key system and
a trumpet-like mouthpiece.

The first one
Sax, born in Belgium in 1814, built his first
'*Sax-o-phone*' when he was in his mid-twenties.
This horn had a range similar to that of the
modern baritone sax. Originally, Sax referred
to it as a bass saxophone. Around 1856 he gave
his instruments their final names, as we know
them today.

Ophicleide.

Military bands
By that time, Sax had developed two saxophone families.

Adolphe Sax (1814–1894).

The largest consisted of six B♭ and E♭ instruments, from the sopranino to the bass. These saxophones were designed to be used in military bands, where their timbre and potential for volume perfectly fit the format.

Symphony orchestras

The other family consisted of four saxes: two in C (soprano and tenor), and two in F (alto and baritone). Their slightly more delicate sound – a result of the higher tuning – was created with the symphony orchestra in mind. However, it took many years for the repertoire to emerge that would earn these instruments a place in orchestral settings.

Alone and a pauper

It was jazz musicians who made the sax really popular, when this style of music began to develop in the early 1900s. Too late for Adolphe Sax, unfortunately: He died in 1894, alone and a pauper, having fought many lawsuits against people who disputed his patents.

Brass and bass clarinets

Besides the saxophone, Sax is also known for his work on various brass instruments (the saxhorns, *e.g.*, the tenor horn and the baritone), and on the bass clarinet.

12. THE FAMILY

Even though saxophones are made of brass, they belong to the family of woodwind instruments, just like clarinets, oboes, and flutes. This chapter covers all the saxophone voices, some saxophone variations of the past, the main other woodwinds, and the electronic family members.

The four most important saxophone voices have been mentioned and described in various chapters in this book. The three others are quite rare. The *sopranino* is even smaller than the soprano, and therefore higher in pitch.

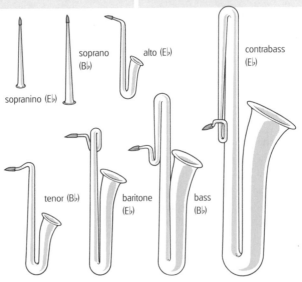

Seven saxophone voices: four in E♭, three in B♭. Together, they almost span the range of a piano.

Bass and contrabass

The *bass saxophone* sounds an octave lower than the tenor.
The rare *contrabass* – the largest of them all – is an octave
lower than the baritone.

A sopranino and a bass saxophone.

C melody

Over the years, many variations on these voices have
been developed. One of the best-known examples is the

C melody, basically a tenor in C. This instrument was extremely popular in the 1920s. Buying one now is usually not a good investment; too many were made to make them very valuable, and it's extremely hard to find matching reeds, mouthpieces, and other parts.

One-handed horns

The same goes for a number of other saxophone variations, most of them built around that same era, such as the soprano sax in C, the sopranino in F, and the *saxello* – a straight B♭ soprano with a bell that pointed toward the audience. Another bell variation was featured on the Conn-O-Sax, a mezzo soprano in F with a bulb-shaped bell that had three additional resonance vents. Conn also made saxophones that could be played with one hand only. These instruments were mainly used in circuses and vaudeville acts.

Plastic saxophone   Tipcode SAX-021

The late Charlie Parker, one of the world's most famous jazz alto players, was known for using a wide variety of horns – and he always sounded like himself, even when he played the white Grafton saxophone, a horn with a plastic (!) body. The Grafton Acrylic Saxophone was available in the early 1950s.

Bamboo

Other saxophone varieties look even less like the original instrument. One example is the Bamboo Jim Brock Sax. The toneholes in the bamboo body are closed with your fingers, just like a recorder, and it uses a regular sax mouthpiece.

OTHER WOODWINDS

The only visible characteristic all woodwinds share is that they consist of a body with various toneholes. Opening and closing these toneholes produces various pitches. This explains why not only wooden instruments (clarinets, oboes, recorders, and so on) are woodwinds, but flutes and saxophones too. Woodwinds also share a certain tone quality or timbre, which is clearly different from that of brasswind instruments (trumpets, trombones, etc.).

Reed instruments

Saxophones and some of the other woodwinds are also classified as *reed instruments*, for obvious reasons. Reed instruments come in two groups: Those with a single reed, such as the clarinet and the sax, and those with a double reed, such as the oboe and the bassoon.

A flute, a clarinet and an oboe.

Clarinet   Tipcode SAX-022

The clarinet is often considered the saxophone's closest relative, as they're both *single-reed instruments*: They have similar mouthpieces with a single *beating reed* – the reed 'beating' against the mouthpiece as it vibrates. The differences between clarinets and saxophones are quite large, though. First, the clarinet has a largely cylindrical body, which makes it sound and blow very differently. Second, the clarinet's register key doesn't make notes sound an octave higher, but a twelfth. Third, its key system is quite different. Fourth, most clarinets have a wooden or synthetic body. Still, many musicians play both instruments.

Oboe and bassoon   Tipcode SAX-023

The oboe, like the sax, has a conical bore. On the other hand, the oboe resembles the clarinet, with its wooden body and its key system. At the same time, it's completely different from those two, because it's a *double-reed instrument*; it has two reeds that vibrate against each other, just like the bassoon, which sounds much lower, and the English horn. This makes it a completely different instrument. Not many musicians play both single- and double-reed instruments.

Flute   Tipcode SAX-024

Flutes were originally made of wood, and many – mainly classical – flutists still prefer wooden instruments to the much more common metal ones. Piccolos, sounding an octave higher, are even more popular in wood, and also available with plastic bodies. The flute's key system has similarities to that of a clarinet and a saxophone. The body is cylindrical, and there's no reed. Versatile woodwind players often play saxophone, clarinet, and flute.

ELECTRONIC WIND INSTRUMENTS

Electronic wind instruments, introduced in the early 1970s, usually have a saxophone-style keywork and mouthpiece. You use them to control and play sounds from sound modules, synthesizers, or other electronic sound sources.

Any sound, seven octaves

Using an electronic wind instrument, you can usually play any type of sound over a seven-octave range, you can play chords, and much more. Lip and wind pressure sensors can be used for different purposes (dynamics, effects, and so on).

MIDI

This is usually done through MIDI, a standardized *musical instrument digital interface*. MIDI allows you to hook up synthesizers to computers, digital sound sources to effect devices and recording equipment, and so on. Electronic wind instruments are often referred to as MIDI Wind Controllers.

Examples

The original American Lyricon served as an example for many later designs. Well-known companies making MIDI wind instruments are Yamaha and Akai. The Synthophone, built inside an alto saxophone body, uses traditional saxophone fingerings.

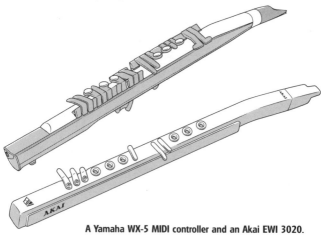

A Yamaha WX-5 MIDI controller and an Akai EWI 3020.

13. HOW THEY'RE MADE

Traditionally, saxophones, mouthpieces, and reeds were made entirely by hand, of course – and some companies still do a lot of things that way. Here's a quick look at what's involved in the various production processes.

Tipcode SAX-025

The body and bell are produced from flat sheets of brass, which are folded double, soldered, and then formed using dies and presses. Some companies still have craftsmen doing this, however, using steel mandrels and wooden hammers. The neck is, simply put, a bent length of pipe.

The traditional way: shaping the tube with a wooden hammer.

The toneholes

To make the toneholes, small holes are drilled into the body and the bell. Then a metal shaft is inserted into the tubing. This *spike* is inset with metal pulling balls, each one matched exactly to the size of the corresponding tonehole. These balls are pulled forcefully through the pre-drilled holes, forming the tonehole chimneys as they go. This technique is known as pulling, drawing, or extruding toneholes.

Posts

Once the toneholes are ready, the posts are mounted on ribs and soldered onto the instrument.

Finishing and assembly

The horn is cleaned and polished extensively before being lacquered or plated. The most common type of finish is an epoxy lacquer, which is baked on the horn. Assembling the horn includes installing the keywork and carefully seating the pads.

Play-testing and adjusting

At the end of the process, the saxophone is play-tested and adjusted. The more expensive the instrument, the more attention will usually be devoted to the final testing and adjusting stage. Most new saxes, however, need an extra shop-adjustment before they're really ready to play.

REEDS AND MOUTHPIECES

Most reeds are made of *Arundo donax*, a type of cane that grows particularly well in southern France (the Var region), but also in South America, Australia, and elsewhere.

Curing

The plants are harvested when they are two to three years old. By then they have usually grown to about 25 feet (eight meters). After harvesting, the cane is dried and cured for a year or more.

By size and into shape   Tipcode SAX-026

The tubes are chopped into short pieces and then sorted by size: larger ones for the big reeds used on baritones, smaller ones for tenors and altos, and so on. The tube lengths are split into four pieces, and each quarter is made into a reed

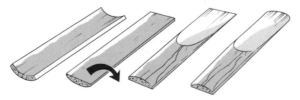

From cane to reed, showing four of the many steps.

using a series of machines and techniques – flattening and sanding, cutting the rough shape, removing the bark, profiling the reed, and cutting the tip. At each stage the reeds are inspected visually, and the bad ones discarded.

Number

A special device measures the resistance of each reed at the tip. The higher the resistance, the harder the reed, and the higher the number it is given. Finally, the reeds are once again inspected thoroughly, stamped, and packed.

Mouthpieces   Tipcode SAX-027

The production process of a mouthpiece mainly consists of boring, reaming, smoothing, flattening, filing, sanding, buffing, polishing, and related treatments. In a series of steps the basic hard rubber or plastic mold is worked to exacting specifications, with tolerances of tens of thousandths of an inch – or even less. Metal mouthpieces, whether they start out as a solid block or as two forged pieces that are soldered together, undergo similar processes. In most companies a number of operations is undertaken by computer-controlled machines; others still require skilled handwork. The final steps include corking and stamping.

14. BRANDS

This chapter offers a brief introduction to the main saxophone brands you'll come across in music stores. At the end, some examples of well-known vintage horns are noted.

There are more saxophone brands than saxophone makers: Some factories make instruments for various brands, and they also supply horns for the private label instruments that are marketed by some of the larger dealers. Also, some companies have their horns largely or entirely made elsewhere – usually in Asian countries.

The larger companies
This chapter starts with brief descriptions of the larger, older companies that make their own horns from start to finish, followed by a section on smaller and newer companies from various countries.

B&S, located in what used to be Eastern Germany, builds saxes and brass instruments in all price ranges and under various names. Codera is one of their main series.

The first Buffet Crampon saxophones were made in 1868, just two years after Adolphe Sax's patent had expired. These higher-priced French instruments are used

---

* Trademarks and/or usernames have been used in this book solely to identify the products or instruments discussed. Such use does not identify endorsement by or affiliation with the trademark owner(s).

mostly by classical musicians. A line of student instruments, marketed as Buffet Crampon Evette, comes from Asia.

 The German company Julius Keilwerth, founded in 1925, produces instruments in the middle-to-high price range. Keilwerth has always made instruments for other brands as well, both from Europe and the US.

 The first Selmer saxophones were made in 1922. Six years later the French company bought the brand name Adolphe Sax Fils (Adolphe Sax's Son, literally). Besides pro saxes, the company also makes various brass instruments. Selmer established its name in America before World War II, at which time the firm cooperated with Buescher.

Selmer ® The American Selmer company evolved from the French collaboration with Buescher. Though sharing the same name, the American and French companies are now independent. Selmer USA focuses on student and intermediate saxes, (formerly) marketed as Selmer Bundy and Selmer Signet, besides making other wind instruments.

YAMAHA ® Yamaha, which started as a one-man organ factory in 1889, is one of the few sax makers that offer horns in all price categories. The first Yamaha saxes were released in 1967. Yamaha also makes all kinds of other instruments, as well as motorbikes, hi-fi equipment, and much more.

YANAGISAWA Yanagisawa began making saxophones in 1954. At present the Japanese company only makes instruments in the higher price range. It's particularly well known for its sopranos, but makes all other voices and special necks as well.

New US-made saxes

Today, only few companies are still producing saxes in the US: The main names are **King**, **Conn** (both UMI brand names), and **Vito**, all focusing on the lower price ranges.

More American brands

Other American companies have their instruments (partly or entirely) made elsewhere but take care of several parts of the production process in house, varying from assembly to adjusting and play-testing the horns.

Some examples of companies that concentrate on the mid or higher price ranges are **Cannonball**, **LA Sax** (well-known for its many colors and designs), and **Guardala** (makes professional mouthpieces too). Others, such as **Antigua Winds**, focus on student and intermediate horns, or on the lower price ranges only (*e.g.*, **Belmonte**, **Blessing**, and **Kohlert**).

Asia

Japan was the first Asian country that started mass production of high quality, affordable instruments. Taiwan followed pretty quickly. Two large Taiwanese companies that make saxophones as well as a host of other instruments are **Dixon** and **Jupiter**.

... and furthermore

Besides the examples mentioned above, European saxes are made and marketed by the Czech company **Amati**; by **Trevor James** from England; by the Dutch **TopTone** company, known for its non-leather pads; and by the Italian companies **Borgani** (since 1872; one of the few companies still making hand-hammered horns), **Grassi**, and **Orsi**. Italy is also known for its pad makers. **Weril** horns are made in Brazil.

VINTAGE SAXES

Vintage saxes, built around or before the 1960s, can be quite valuable – but others aren't a good investment at all. Some series, for example, have known good and bad years; bad horns have been made in good years too; and not every horn has stood the test of time (or the sometimes indelicate techniques of the people who owned it) equally well. Please refer to specialized literature and contact saxophone stores for additional information, and for listings of serial numbers that show you exactly when a sax was built. These listings can also be found on the Internet (see page 127).

Old American horns

Pretty much every 'old' American sax maker produced one or more horns that are still in demand. Some of these names may be found on new instruments too.

- **Conn**, for instance, founded in 1888 as the first American sax manufacturer, became well known for saxophones such as the Naked Lady, the Ladyface, the Connquerer, the 10-M, and the Chu Berry.
- **King's** claims to fame were the Zephyr and the richly engraved Super 20, among others.
- Ferdinand August **Buescher**, who first worked for Conn, later produced his own instruments. The 400 and the 1940s Aristocrat are famous models.
- **Martin** was well-known for its soldered (rather than drawn) toneholes. The Committee and the Magna are some of the best known models of this brand. Martin also made a sax with mother-of-pearl keys all over, known as the Typewriter.

Selmer

Examples of well-known vintage Selmers are the Cigar Cutter, the Super Action, and the Balanced Action. Their key mechanisms, compared to American-made saxes from that period, were quite advanced. The most famous sax of all time is probably the Selmer Mark VI, which was made from 1954 until the early 1970s. A good Mark VI, especially when made in the early 1960s or before, easily costs as much or more than a new professional horn.

Old for less

Other older saxes include popular student or intermediate instruments that offer decent quality for much less money. Some examples from the late 1950s until the late 1970s are the Martin Handcraft, the King Cleveland, the Selmer Bundy, the Conn PanAm, and the Conn USA. Instruments from that era by Armstrong and Vito may serve you well too, as will the King 613 and the Conn 16M.

VINTAGE MOUTHPIECES

Also, there's a market for older mouthpieces, some of which are highly prized by saxophonists who want that traditional, vintage sound – and they may cost as much or more than a new one. A few examples are old Berg Larsens, Otto Link mouthpieces from the 1950s, Dukoffs from the 1940s, and Brilharts from that same era. A tip: Just as new mouthpieces don't always work well with vintage saxophones, old mouthpieces may not fit new horns either (see page 57).

GLOSSARY AND INDEX

This glossary contains short definitions of the main saxophone-related terms. The numbers refer to the pages where they are covered in more detail.

Action *(44)* The mechanical 'feel' of your sax.

Adjustment *(25, 44–45, 111)* A poorly adjusted sax is hard to play.

Altissimo register *(13)* Higher notes than the keys of your sax may seem to allow you. Also known as *top tones* or *high harmonics*.

Alto saxophone *(14)* The most popular saxophone voice.

American cut *(74)* A reed with a slightly thicker tip and less heart, as opposed to a French cut reed. See also: *French file cut*.

Articulated G♯, Automatic G♯ *(40)* Opens the G♯ vent when low C♯, B, or B♭ are used.

Baffle *(59, 65)* A 'bump' on the inside of the mouthpiece, making for a more aggressive, piercing sound. Also called *wedge*.

Bari, baritone saxophone *(15–16)* The lowest-sounding of the four most common sax voices.

Bell, bell keys *(5, 6, 39, 42)* The flared opening of the sax. *Bell keys* are the keys that open or close the toneholes in the bell.

Body *(4–6, 33–36)* If you remove the neck, the bow, and the bell, you are left with the body.

Bore 1. *(34)* The internal dimensions of the mouthpiece, neck, body, bow, and bell. 2. *(59)* The end of a mouthpiece, into which

Dutch rush or reed rush.

the neck fits. 3. Another word for chamber. See: *Chamber.*

Bow *(4)* The U-bend between body and bell.

Brace 1. *(37)* Reinforcement, connecting the body to the bell. 2. *(93)* A suspender-like neckstrap.

Cap *(80)* Mouthpiece and reed protector.

Cases and gig bags *(90–92)* A sax is a very delicate instrument that needs proper protection when being transported.

Chamber *(59, 64–66)* The internal space of a mouthpiece. Also referred to as *bore.*

Conical bore *(6, 34, 108)* A sax has a conical bore: It gets wider toward the bell. See also: *Bore.*

Crook See: *Neck, neckpipe.*

Doubler *(68, 81, 94)* Someone who plays more than one (wind) instrument, *i.e.,* sax and clarinet, or sax and flute, or all three.

Dutch rush *(79)* A plant that grows in swamps, used for adjusting reeds. Also known as *reed rush.*

Ebonite See: *Hard rubber.*

Embouchure *(19, 21, 48, 58)* The way you use your lips, jaws, tongue, and all the muscles around them when playing a wind instrument.

Facing 1. *(59, 63–64)* The area where the mouthpiece curves away from the reed. Also called *lay.* 2. The underside of a reed.

French cut See: *American cut.*

French file cut *(74)* Special way of cutting reeds, making for a more open, brighter sound. Not to be confused with *French cut.*

Front F *(12, 43)* A key to easily reach a high E, F, or F♯. Also referred to as *quick F* or *forked F.*

Hard rubber *(68–70)* What most mouthpieces are made of. Also known as *rubber* or *ebonite.*

High F# *(12, 39)* Special key to play high F#.

High pitch, HP *(55)* Some older saxes have a higher standard tuning.

Hook 1. *(93)* The hook on the neckstrap. 2. *(44)* The supporting hook for your right thumb.

Insurance *(96)* Smart.

Intonation *(35, 48–49, 56, 85)* A sax with bad intonation will be difficult, if not impossible, to play in tune. A player who has bad intonation will play out of tune even on the best saxophone.

Key cups *(6, 44, 47)* The cups holding the pads that cover the toneholes.

Key height *(44–45, 49)* The distance a key opens.

Key risers *(43)* Affordable way to raise keys that are too low for your hands.

Key system *(39–45)* The saxophone's mechanism.

Keys *(4–6, 8–12, 39–43, 54)* Keys allow you to open and close the saxophone's toneholes.

Lay See: *Facing*.

Leaks *(6, 38, 48, 54, 55, 100–101)* A leaky sax doesn't respond well and will probably play out of tune too.

Ligature *(5, 6, 70–71, 83)* Holds the reed in place.

Little finger keys *(5, 9–10, 41)* The *pinkie keys* or *touch plates* that are operated with your left and right little fingers are also referred to as *plateau keys* or *table keys*, and the two groups of keys are known as *plateaus* or *tables*.

Microphones *(95–96)* Vocal microphones work great for sax players. There are also dedicated sax mics that attach to the bell of the instrument.

Mouthpiece *(5, 6, 37, 58–70)* The most crucial part of the instrument, together with the reed.

Mouthpiece cushion, pad, patch *(68)* Reduces the vibration of a (metal) mouthpiece against your teeth. Also used to protect mouthpieces against bite marks.

Mute *(21–22)* Most sax mutes are not very effective, due to the nature of the instrument.

Neck, neck pipe *(5, 6, 34, 36–37, 53–54)* The tube that connects mouthpiece and body. Also referred to as *gooseneck* or (British) *crook*.

Neck cork *(54, 87)* Cork sleeve at the end of the neck. Also referred to as *tuning cork*.

Neckstrap *(92–94)* Comes in a wide variety, from basic ones to harnesses.

Octave key, octave vents *(8, 11, 12, 40, 56–57)* The octave key 'automatically' opens the lower or the upper octave vent, depending on the note that you finger. Also known as *register key*: When you use it, you move to a higher register.

Pads *(6, 45–47, 98–99)* Pads seal the toneholes.

Pad saver *(88–89)* A long, plush-covered rod, used to reduce the moisture in your instrument.

Palm keys *(5, 10, 42, 43)* Set of keys operated with the palm or the fingers of your left hand.

Pearl keys *(9)* Keys with pearl inlays. See: *Keys*.

Pinkie keys See: *Little finger keys*.

Plateau, plateau keys See: *Little finger keys*.

Post construction *(38)* See: *Rib construction*.

Posts *(38)* Hold the key mechanism in place.

Quick F See: *Front F*.

Rails *(59, 64)* The three edges (tip and side rails) of the mouthpiece's window.

Range *(15)* The distance from the lowest to the highest notes on the instrument.

Reed, reed instrument, reed player *(5, 6, 60–63, 69, 72–81)* The reed is the part that vibrates as you play, setting the air in motion and producing the sound. A good reed should match both your way of playing and your mouthpiece. Saxophones are *reeds* or *reed instruments*, and saxophonists are sometimes referred to as *reed players* – just like clarinetists, for example.

Reed adjustment *(78–81)* Dull, squeaking, shrill, or uneven reeds can sometimes be adjusted.

Reed guard *(88)* Protective holder for reeds.

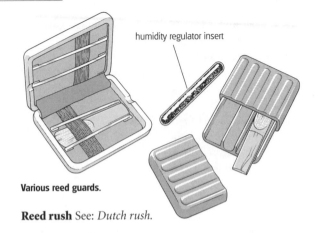

humidity regulator insert

Various reed guards.

Reed rush See: *Dutch rush.*

Register *(12–13)* The range of the saxophone is often broken down into three registers: low (all notes without octave key), middle (with octave key), and high (with octave key plus side keys).

Register key See: *Octave key.*

Resonator *(6, 45, 46)* Metal or plastic disc on the inside of a pad.

Rib construction, ribbed construction *(38)* Saxes with a rib(bed) construction have the posts attached to metal strips, rather than directly to the body (i.e., *post mounting*).

Sax, Adolphe *(102–103)* The instrument's inventor.

Secondhand instruments *(27–29, 52–57)* Buying tips for used instruments.

Side keys *(5, 10)* Set of keys on the lower right-hand side of the instrument, used to play high notes and trills.

Side rails See: *Rails.*

Soprano saxophone *(14, 34)* The highest pitched of the four most common saxes.

Spatula keys, spatulas *(10, 43)* Spatula-shaped keys. Used to refer to little finger keys and other keys.

Springs *(8, 44, 97)* Needle springs make the keys return to their original positions after you've played them.

Stack *(10)* To some, the low stack refers to the bottom (right hand) half of the key mechanism, and the high stack to the other half. To others, low and high stack refer to the right- and left-hand little finger keys, respectively.

Table 1. *(73)* The flat underside of the reed. 2. The flat part of the mouthpiece on which the reed lies. 3. The two groups of little finger keys or *table keys*. See: *Little finger keys.*

Tenor saxophone *(14–15)* One of the two most commonly played saxes.

Thumb hook, thumb rest *(5, 8, 43–44)* Thumb hooks (right thumb) may be adjustable. Thumb rests (left thumb) aren't.

Thumb saver *(44)* A soft sleeve to cover the thumb hook.

Tilting keys *(41)* Little finger keys that tilt toward the key that's being played. Special feature.

Tip opening *(59, 62–63)* The distance between the tip of the reed and the tip of the mouthpiece.

Toneholes *(4–6, 38)* The holes in the sax, also known as sound holes or vents.

Touch plates See: *Little finger keys.*

Transposing instruments *(17–18)* On a transposing instrument, the note that sounds (concert pitch) is different from the one you finger. The fingered C on an alto sax sounds an E♭ concert pitch; the fingered C on a tenor saxophone sounds a B♭.
Non-transposing instruments (the piano and the flute, for example) play in *concert pitch.*

Tuning *(84–87)* Adjusting the position of the mouthpiece so that the instrument plays at the correct pitch – in tune with other instruments, and with itself.

Tuning cork See: *Neck cork.*

U-bend See: *Bow.*

Vintage saxes *(28, 56–57, 115–117)* Good vintage saxes are much in demand.

Wedge See: *Baffle.*

Window *(59)* Mouthpiece's rectangular opening, covered by the reed.

Woodwind instrument *(32, 106–108)* Saxophones belong to the family of woodwind instruments, even though they're made of metal.

TIPCODE LIST

The Tipcodes in this book offer easy access to short movies, photo series, soundtracks, and other additional information at www.tipbook.com. For your convenience, the Tipcodes in this Tipbook have been listed below.

WANT TO KNOW MORE?

Tipbooks supply you with basic information on the instrument of your choice and everything that comes with it. Of course there's a lot more to be found on all subjects you came across on these pages. A selection of magazines, books, websites, and newsgroups, as well as some background on the makers of the Tipbook series.

MAGAZINES

Some magazines that offer additional information on saxophones and saxophone playing:

- *The Saxophone Journal*, Dorn Publications Inc., phone (508) 359-1015, dornpub@dornpub.com, www.dornpub.com.
- *Windplayer*, phone (310) 456-5813, info@windplayer.com, www.windplayer.com.
- *Band & Orchestra Product News*, phone (516) 767-2500, www.bandandorchestra.com.

BOOKS

Most books listed below cover the instrument itself and often discuss other subjects such as playing techniques, history, and repertoire at greater length.

- *The Art of Saxophone Playing*, by Larry Teal (Summy Birchard Inc., New Jersey, USA, 1963; 111 pages; ISBN 0 87487 7).
- *Saxophone – Yehudi Menuhin Music Guides*, by Paul Harvey (Kahn & Averill, London, 1995; 149 pages; ISBN 1 871082 53 6).
- *The Cambridge Companion to the Saxophone* (Cambridge Companions to Music), by Richard Ingham (Editor)

(Cambridge University Press, 1999; ISBN 0 52159 348 4).

- *Celebrating the Saxophone*, by Paul Lindemeyer (Hearst Books, published by William Morrow & Co., Inc. 1996; 96 pages; ISBN 0 688135 188).
- *The Saxophone*, by Lawrence Gwozdz (Egon Publishers, England, 1987; ISBN 0 905 858 40 9). A translation of the first comprehensive treatise on the instrument, *Das Saxophon*, by Jaap Kool, first published in 1931.
- If you want to find out about the instrument's inventor, you can consult *Adolphe Sax 1814–1894 – His Life and Legacy*, by Wally Horwood (Egon Publishers, England, 1980; 214 pages; ISBN 0 905858 18 2).
- Some of the books above also cover adjusting reeds. A specialized publication is *Perfect a Reed … and Beyond*, by Ben Armato (private publication; 1996; 43 pages; available at major US music dealers).
- *Sax and His Saxophone*, by Leon Kochnitzky (University of Louisville; 1985; ISBN 9 991 08 32 6).

SAXOPHONISTS' ORGANIZATIONS
Magazines and newsletters are also published by various national and international saxophonists' organizations. These groups promote saxophone playing by organizing workshops and congresses (*e.g.*, the international World Saxophone Congress, held every three years, as well as national congresses and conferences), and by providing information to and establishing contacts between players at all levels, and so on.

- The North American Saxophone Alliance (NASA; www.saxalliance.org) publishes *NASA Update* and *The Saxophone Symposium*. For membership information: membership@saxalliance.org.
- The European Clarinet and Saxophone Society (www.eurocass.org) publishes *Eurocass Magazine.*
- The Clarinet and Saxophone Society of Great Britain (phone +44 (0)20 8979 6064, membership@cassgb.co.uk, www.cassgb.co.uk) publishes *Clarinet & Saxophone.*
- The Queensland Clarinet & Saxophone Society (phone +61 (0)7 3341 8086, enquiries@clarinet-saxophone.asn.au, www.clarinet-saxophone.asn.au) publishes *The Australian Clarinet & Saxophone Magazine.*

INTERNET

The Internet offers lots of advice and information about saxes, players, reeds, mouthpieces, and more. The following sites are good starting points, offering both information and links to other sites.

- *The International Saxophone Home Page* (ISHP; also features the Saxophone Buyer's Guide by Webmaster Jason DuMars): www.saxophone.org.
- *Bubba's Saxophone Links*: www.mindspring.com/~mgm/saxlinks.html.
- *The Saxophone Site* (Sax on the Web): www.geocities.com/saxontheweb.
- To add your own links to a long list of sites, go to members.aol.com/saxring.
- Two interesting newsgroups are alt.music.saxophone and The Sax FAQ (www.bobrk.com/saxfaq or rec.music.makers.saxophone).

OTHER TIPBOOKS

Among the other Tipbooks that you may find of interest is *Tipbook Music on Paper*, which tells you basically everything you need to know about sheet music and music theory. This book teaches you to read music in a couple of chapters. Other Tipbook titles that may be of interest for sax players are *Clarinet* and *Flute*, for example (see page 132).

ABOUT THE MAKERS

Journalist and musician Hugo Pinksterboer, author of The Tipbook Series, has published hundreds of interviews, articles, and instrument, video, CD, and book reviews for Dutch and international music magazines. He is the author of *The Cymbal Book*, and has also written and developed a wide variety of manuals and courses, both for musicians and for non-musicians.

Illustrator, designer, and musician Gijs Bierenbroodspot has worked as an art director for a wide variety of magazines and developed numerous ad campaigns. While searching for information about saxophone mouthpieces, he got the idea for this series of books on music and musical instruments. He is responsible for the design and illustrations for all of the Tipbooks. He has also found a good mouthpiece, in the meantime.

ESSENTIAL DATA

In the event of your instrument being stolen or lost, or if you decide to sell it, it's useful to have all the relevant data at hand. Here are two pages to list everything you need – for the insurance, for the police, for a prospective buyer or just for yourself.

INSURANCE

Company:

Phone: Fax:

E-mail:

Agent:

Phone: Fax:

E-mail:

Policy number: Premium:

INSTRUMENTS AND ACCESSORIES

Brand and type:

Serial number: Price:

Date of purchase:

Purchased from:

Phone: Fax:

E-mail:

Brand and type:

Serial number: Price:

Date of purchase:

Purchased from:

Phone: Fax:

E-mail:

MOUTHPIECES

Brand and type:

Date of purchase: Price:

Purchased from:

Phone: Fax:

E-mail:

Brand and type:

Date of purchase: Price:

Purchased from:

Phone: Fax:

E-mail:

REEDS

Brand, type, number:

Price:

Comments:

Brand, type, number:

Price:

Comments:

Brand, type, number:

Price:

Comments:

Brand, type, number:

Price:

Comments:

Brand, type, number:

Price:

Comments:

ADDITIONAL NOTES

TIPBOOK SERIES
MUSIC AND MUSICAL INSTRUMENTS*
Released

Tipbook Acoustic Guitar
Tipbook Clarinet
Tipbook Drums
Tipbook Piano
Tipbook Trumpet & Trombone
Tipbook Violin & Viola
Tipbook Saxophone
Tipbook Flute & Piccolo

Expected in 2002

Tipbook Cello
Tipbook Electric Guitar and Bass Guitar
Tipbook Home Keyboard and Digital Piano
Tipbook Music on Paper – Basic Theory
Tipbook Vocals

TBA

Tipbook Accordion
Tipbook Amplifiers and Effects
Tipbook Background Brass
Tipbook Composing and Arranging
Tipbook Home Recording
Tipbook Improvisation
Tipbook MIDI
Tipbook Music for Children
Tipbook Music on Paper part II
Tipbook Oboe and Bassoon
Tipbook Percussion
Tipbook Synthesizer and Sampler

*Titles subject to change.

Want to know what's available today?
Take a look at www.tipbook.com.